Royal Horses

Also by Judith Campbell:

THE QUEEN RIDES
ANNE, PORTRAIT OF A PRINCESS
PRINCESS ANNE AND HER HORSES
ELIZABETH AND PHILIP
ROYALTY ON HORSEBACK
ANNE AND MARK
CHARLES: A PRINCE OF OUR TIMES
QUEEN ELIZABETH II
THE ROYAL PARTNERS

Royal Horses

Judith Campbell

New English Library

Copyright ©1983 by Judith Campbell
Introduction copyright©Brough Scott 1983

First published in Great Britain
in 1983 by New English Library,
Mill Road, Dunton Green,
Sevenoaks, Kent.
Editorial office:
47 Bedford Square,
London WC1B 3DP.

Design: Ian Hughes

Text setting by:
Hewer Text Composition Services

Printed and bound in Italy

British Library Cataloguing in
Publication Data
Campbell, Judith
   Royal horses.
   1. Horsesports—Great Britain
   2. Great Britain—Kings and
        rulers—Sports
   I. Title
   798'.092'2   SF294.2

ISBN: 0 450 06001 2

Contents

Introduction by Brough Scott   ix

1   A History of the Royal Stables   11

2   The Work of the Royal Mews   25

3   Queen Elizabeth: Her Riding Career   41

4   Royal Bloodstock   57

5   Prince Philip: Polo Enthusiast   69

6   Carriage Driving   79

7   Royal Racing   97

8   Charles: The Prince and his Horses   113

9   Competition Riding   127

10   Princess Anne: Olympic Rider   141

11   Anne and Mark: Eventing Successes   159

12   Equestrianism: The Family Tradition   181

A Final Word   189

List of Illustrations

Page
10 The Prince and Princess of Wales returning from St. Paul's Cathedral on Royal Wedding Day, July 29 1981.
13 Coronation Day, June 2 1953. The State Coach bearing the Queen and the Duke of Edinburgh passing the crowds on its way to Westminster Abbey.
14 The Queen at the Trooping the Colour. Behind her rides Prince Philip and Prince Charles.
19 The Glass Coach bearing the Queen Mother and Princess Margaret leaves Buckingham Palace on Prince Philip and Princess Elizabeth's Wedding Day, November 20 1947.
21 The Queen and Prince Philip passing schoolchildren lining the route to Royal Ascot in a horse-drawn open carriage in June 1981.
23 A view from the crowd of the procession for the State Opening of Parliament.
24 The King's Coachmen busy cleaning semi-state harness in the Royal Mews.
26 A view inside the stables of the Royal Mews at Buckingham Palace.
27 Final preparations are made on the Glass Coach before setting off to take Lady Diana to St. Paul's on Royal Wedding Day, July 29 1981.
29 Coronation Day, June 2 1953. A final inspection of the grooms, who walk each side of the postilions, shown with the crooked sticks which they use to keep an even pull on the traces.
31 top – Coronation Day, June 1953. The State Coach postilions.
   bottom – A display of coaches which are housed in the Royal Mews. Left to right: the Balmoral Sociable, the French Charabanc, the Irish State Coach and two State Landaus.
33 A fine view of the State Coach bearing Queen Elizabeth II passing Eros on Coronation Day, June 2 1953.
34 top – The Gold State Coach used for every Coronation since George IV.
   bottom left – Detail from one of the panels on the side of the Coach painted by the Florentine artist, Cipriani.
   bottom right – Close-up of one of the superb gilt figures adorning the coach.
39 The postilions in full livery stand before the Glass Coach on the Prince and Princess of Wales' Wedding Day, July 1981.
40 Princess Elizabeth and her favourite pony, Greylight, on her thirteenth birthday.
42 Queen Elizabeth riding side-saddle on Burmese.
44 far left – The Queen enjoying a gallop at Ascot on her horse, Betsy.
   centre left – Catching up with other members of the party.
   left – Badminton Great Park. The Queen and Princess Margaret out on their morning ride.
   below – The Queen on Betsy. Princess Margaret in the background is riding with their host, Lord Beaufort.
47 Queen Elizabeth attending the third day of the Annual Horse Trials at Badminton in 1959.
49 top – The Queen comforts Burmese after the dramatic events at the Trooping the Colour ceremony in June 1981.
   bottom – Princess Elizabeth showing her command of side-saddle riding in 1947 at the first Trooping the Colour since the War.
50 The Queen, Prince Philip and Prince Charles at the Trooping the Colour ceremony.
51 top – The pageantry of the Guards marching with the Queen at the Trooping the Colour.
   bottom – The Queen enjoying a relaxed canter through the grounds at Balmoral.
53 The Queen riding Burmese at the Trooping the Colour in the uniform of Colonel-in-Chief of the Irish Guards. Behind her, Prince Charles, Major H. P. D. Massey (Field Officer) and the Earl of Westmorland (Master of Horse).
55 The Queen riding Burmese and her guest, American President Ronald Reagan, up on Centenial, set off on their hour long ride in Windsor Home Park in June 1982. Mr Reagan was the first American president to be a guest of a British monarch since 1918.
56 The Queen and the Manager of the Royal Studs at Sandringham, Mr Michael Oswald, admire her Classic winning filly, Highclere.
58 The Queen and Prince Philip riding in an Ascot Landau in the sunshine at the races.
59 left – Princess Elizabeth pats Monaveen after a magnificent win in the Queen Elizabeth Steeplechase at Hurst Park in December 1949.
   right – The Queen with her Ascot winner Aureole in 1954.
60 Doutelle after winning the 2000 Guineas Trial Stakes at Kempton Park in 1957. The Queen, Princess Margaret, her trainer Captain Boyd Rochfort and her racing manager Captain C. Moore, look on with delight.
62 The Queen with Lester Piggott at Goodwood Race Course in 1964.
63 The Queen, Prince Philip and the Queen Mother looking over the field at the Epsom Derby.
65 Australia Fair, a two-year-old race horse presented to the Queen by the Australian Government, arriving at the Newmarket Stables of William Hastings-Bass.
67 Another triumphant day at Ascot for the Queen.
68 Prince Philip capturing the ball during a polo match at Cowdray Park in July 1967.
70 top – 1964. Prince Philip and Prince Charles practising together on Smith's Lawn near Windsor Castle.
   bottom – Prince Philip displaying fine control of his pony in a game at Windsor in July 1968.
72 The Queen moves among members of the public stamping down divots kicked up by the ponies during the Royal Windsor Polo Tournament in June 1955.
73 The Queen presenting a tankard to the Duke of Edinburgh – a member of the winning Friar Park team in an invitation polo match against Silver Leys on Smith's Lawn in Windsor Great Park in June 1957.
74 One of Prince Philip's last games at Smith's Lawn.
75 Prince Philip chatting with the Queen after umpiring a polo game at Windsor.
78 Prince Philip competes in the Marathon at the 1981 National Carriage Driving Championships in Windsor Great Park.

81   top – Prince Philip competing with the Queen's team of bays in the dressage section of the International Driving Grand Prix at the Royal Windsor Horse Show at Home Park in May 1981.
      bottom – September 1981 at Windsor Great Park. Prince Philip and the timekeeper, Mrs Pauline Booth-Jones, negotiate the pond in Section A of the Marathon at the National Carriage Driving Championships.

82   left – Prince Philip in immaculate turnout for the dressage section of a competition.
      right – Prince Philip maneouvring his four-in-hand through the sandpit obstacle during a Marathon.

83   Prince Philip showing his skill in a smooth turn.

84   A sunny day for Prince Philip in the International Driving Grand Prix in May 1982.

86   Prince Philip with his team at the Windsor Horse Show.

93   The Duke of Edinburgh taking Mrs Nancy Reagan on a carriage drive through Windsor Home Park in June 1982.

94–95   A decade before the Russian invasion of Afghanistan Prince Philip's horse interests and excellent photography enabled him to capture for posterity pictures of top-notch Afghan horsemen playing buzkashi. This was the rough, tough equestrian sport where whips could be used on opponents, but never on their horses, and the 'ball' was usually a headless goat. Pictures from the Duke of Edinburgh's own collection.

96   King George VI and Queen Elizabeth attending the Oaks at Epsom on May 25 1950.

98   The Queen Mother at the Cheltenham Races in March 1982.

101   The Queen Mother with Devon Loch after the 1956 Grand National.

102   A near miss at the Ascot Races for the Queen Mother's horse.

104   The Queen Mother's horse Laffy after a triumphant win at the Ulster Harp National at Downpatrick on April 6 1962.

105   Makaldar after racing in the Champion Hurdle Challenge Cup at Cheltenham in 1967.

108   The Queen Mother at Sandown Park with her laughing horse, Special Cargo, after winning the Alanbrooke Memorial Handicap Chase in March 1981.

111   top left – The Queen Mother at Badminton Horse Trials.
      top right – Watching progress with the crowds at Badminton.
      bottom – The Queen Mother inspecting the course at Cheltenham.

112   Prince Charles on his favourite horse Allibar in the Club Amateur Riders' Handicap Steeplechase race at Ludlow in October 1980.

113   The young Prince Charles on Greensleeves and Princess Anne on William riding at Windsor in 1957.

114   Prince Charles with his polo pony at Smith's Lawn, Windsor.

115   Prince Charles and Princess Anne competing in the Ascot Gymkhana in April 1963.

116   Prince Charles, aged fourteen, riding his pony San Quinina in a practice polo game on Smith's Lawn.

118   Prince Charles in fierce competition for the ball in a match at Windsor.

121   Prince Charles with the Quorn Hunt on November 15 1980 – his birthday.

122   Prince Charles mounts his pony before a polo game in Oxfordshire.

123   Prince Charles passing villagers on his way to join the Cheshire Hunt.

126   Prince Charles rides Collingwood in a cross-country team event in the Cotswolds.

129   Lady Diana with Nick Gaselee, who trains Good Prospect for Prince Charles, at Sandown in the spring of 1981.

130   Charles making good progress on Candlewick in a cross-country team event at Cirencester.

131   Prince Charles competing in a North Warwickshire Hunt team cross-country event.

133   left – Good Prospect.
      right – Prince Charles on Good Prospect taking one of the early fences in fine style before his fall at the eighteenth at Sandown in March 1981.

135   Prince Charles rewards his horse with sugar lumps after competing in a Quorn Hunt Cross-Country Event.

138   Prince Charles looking relaxed and happy while practising polo in Deauville, France.

140   January 1957. Prince Charles and Princess Anne at the West Norfolk Hunt's meet at Harpley. With them is Major R. Hoare, the Acting Master and Huntsman.

143   The young Princess Anne at the Windsor Horse Show in May 1961.

144   left – Princess Anne on Purple Star during the Showjumping Section of the Windsor Horse Trials in April 1968.
      right – Royal Spectators. Prince Philip and Prince Andrew watching Princess Anne competing in the Dressage Section.

146   The Queen and Princess Anne watching competitors during the Eridge Horse Trials in August 1968. Alison Oliver is standing on the left.

151   Princess Anne and Prince Charles enjoying a ride at Balmoral.

153   Princess Anne and Doublet taking one of the cross-country obstacles in the Crookham Horse Trials at Tweseldown Racecourse in March 1972.

154   Princess Anne out riding on Purple Star in 1969.

157   Princess Anne competing on Doublet in the Calia Insurance Mid-Summer Dressage Championship at Barham Park, Wembley in July 1973.

158   Princess Anne on Goodwill and Captain Mark Philips on Columbus at the Badminton Horse Trials.

160   Captain Mark Phillips and Lincoln after winning the Badminton Horse Trials for the fourth time in April 1981.

163   left – Immaculately turned out Captain Mark Phillips reassuring his horse before a competition.
      right – Mid-flight. Princess Anne on Columbus taking an obstacle on the cross-country course at the Windsor Horse Trials in April 1972.

165   Captain Mark Phillips on Great Ovation competing at the Amberley Horse Show, Cirencester in March 1973.

170   Princess Anne with Doublet at the Burghley Horse Trials.

173   Captain Mark Phillips taking part in the Dressage Competition at Badminton on the Queen's horse Columbus in April 1980.

175   A dramatic picture of Captain Mark Phillips taking a difficult jump on Classic Lines at Badminton in June 1982.

179   Princess Anne and Captain Mark Phillips leaving Badminton House Stables, the Princess looking elegant in competition dressage outfit.

180   Jockey Eph Smith touches his cap to the Queen and Princess Margaret in the paddock after his victory on Snow Cat in the Rous Memorial Stakes at Ascot in 1958.

182   left – Princess Margaret pats prizewinner Windsor Romany Lass at the National Pony Show in 1950.
      right – The Duke and Duchess of Gloucester riding with the Woodland Pytchley Hunt in November 1935.

184   Princess Alexandra presenting the cup to the winner of the Children's Pony Event at the Aldershot Horse Show in 1946.

187   Prince Edward riding Reneau out in the grounds at Badminton.

188   An informal portrait of Princess Anne and Captain Mark Phillips at Locko Park near Derby in August 1980.

191   The Queen and her sister Princess Margaret chatting happily during the Badminton Horse Trials in 1957.

Acknowledgements

Most grateful thanks are due to The Queen and Queen Elizabeth The Queen Mother for giving me access to their horses and stables, and to Prince Philip, Prince Charles, Princess Anne, and Princess Michael of Kent for telling me in person about their various horse interests. I am also most appreciative for the helpful replies to written questions about their own and their families' riding, provided by Princess Margaret, Princess Alice and the Duke and Duchess of Gloucester, Princess Alexandra, and the Duke and Duchess of Kent.

I also wish to thank Sir John Miller for his invaluable assistance, and Lt. Col. Sir Martin Gilliat, Mr Michael Oswald and Mr Fulke Walwyn for their most helpful information.

Credits

The pictures on pages 68, 70 top and bottom, 143, 144 left and right, 146, 151, 154, 157, 163 left and right, and 165 are reproduced by courtesy of Fox Photos Ltd.

Grateful thanks to the Duke of Edinburgh for permission to reproduce his Afghanistan photographs on pages 94 and 95.

Grateful thanks to the Royal Stud for permission to reproduce the photograph on page 56.

Grateful thanks to the John Topham Picture Library for permission to reproduce all other black and white photographs and for all their help.

Grateful thanks to the Tim Graham Picture Library for permission to reproduce all other colour photographs and thanks for all their help.

Introduction by Brough Scott

Maybe history doesn't repeat itself but read this book and you will have to think that if equestrianism were suddenly banned today's royal family would, like Richard III, gladly trade their 'kingdom for a horse'.

We have all got so used to the many other activities of the House of Windsor – those hand-shaking, ship launching, ribbon cutting, world addressing public duties – that we can forget the enormously deep 'horsey' roots in this particular family tree.

How many teams can go back eight hundred years to find a direct ancestor (Richard I) very thrilled with the arrival of two hot blooded 'running horses' from The Crusades? Almost three hundred years ago Queen Anne was 'the mightiest huntress of her age'. One of the Prince Regent's proudest achievements was to do the one hundred and eight mile round trip to Brighton in just ten saddle sore hours. King George V had his favourite pony Jock follow his funeral cortège while another Jock, a dour looking Scottish deer pony had on his photo a royal inscription from our present Queen: 'To Jock who taught me more than any other horse . . .'.

While Judith Campbell is too discreet to indulge in too many eye-catching royal quotes it is obvious from the text that this is a book of rare privilege. It takes you through the Queen's subtle understanding of all her horses from stallions to stag carriers, and to Prince Philip's extraordinary involvement, often with ceremonial horses, in carriage driving now that he claims to be 'too old and decrepit to play polo'.

We are reminded of the astonishing achievements of Princess Anne in becoming European Champion and Sports Personality of 1971 on Doublet, a horse originally bred as a royal polo pony. And we are told that when she first started schooling Columbus it was 'a family joke' that she should keep him out of sight from her grandmother lest he be whisked away as a steeplechaser. We are hinted more excitements in that sphere from Prince Charles, and even have such exotic vignettes as Princess Michael spending six months on a cattle ranch in South West Africa.

Over any year the royal family get involved in more Travels than Gulliver ever dreamed of. Someday surely they will land up, like him, in the land of the Houyhnhnms, where only the horses are wise. Like almost everywhere else 'The Royals' will be amongst friends.

Chapter One

A History of the Royal Stables

BEAUTY WAS one of the ingredients of that unforgettable day of July 29 1981 when the Prince of Wales married his lovely princess in St Paul's Cathedral. It was an occasion that deserved a beautiful setting and few could deny that the total of 348 horses involved made a major contribution to the overall pageantry. There were the police horses, 124 of them on duty all day, one acting as 'pointer' to the whole procession, another as 'pointer' with four leaders for the bride's procession, and two more with pride of place either side of her carriage. There were the superbly turned-out mounts of the four divisions of the Sovereign's Escorts of the Household Cavalry that, including two Standard parties, amounted to 160 horses. Above all there were the 34 horses from the Royal Mews, impeccably presented and well behaved, decked out in their magnificent state trappings and drawing the elegant carriages that are themselves clippings from history. They were accompanied by outriders, and controlled by coachmen and postillions with attendant footmen, all in full state livery.

As a nation the British excel at ceremonial occasions that, like the monarchy itself, represent bonds of continuity, linking the historic past with the present and acting as a bridge to the future. Although these occasions are so well done that they appear gloriously effortless, they do entail an army of people working away like beavers for months beforehand. It is probable that if the entire procession had taken the form of a motorcade, like that comprising sleek black cars and motor-cycle outriders which brought the VIPs from overseas along that royal wedding route, the whole affair might have been considerably easier to organise. Timings and distances that have to be worked out to the second, to the yard, for a horse-drawn procession at the trot, would surely be easier to calculate if the horsepower were mechanised. Security for the royal family and their guests would also be less complicated. Fortunately for the British public, overseas visitors, and all those for whom the spectacle of historic ceremonial is meaningful, the royal family believe tradition is important, see no reason to alter anything to do with the monarchy that 'still works', and are all true horse-lovers.

The Prince and Princess of Wales returning from St Paul's Cathedral on Royal Wedding Day, July 29 1981.

Quite apart from the royal family's personal feelings, there is the significant historical connection between monarchy and horses stretching back into the dim past. In the Middle East and parts of Europe

and Asia the association was formed hundreds of years before the birth of Christ. In England the link was forged later, partly because the Saxons continued to fight solely on foot long after most other overseas communities had taken to combat on horseback. Another cogent reason could be that until the eleventh century English horses were of the small Celtic pony type, quite unlike the animals of the Middle East or the larger chargers later introduced with the House of Normandy. And 'however handsome a man may be, he appears insignificant on a little horse . . .'.

Prestige was to play a big part in the connection between throne and horse but it was a question of dignity combined with practicality. When horses became vital to English warfare and in the days when the king led his troops into battle there was more than one reason for him to be better mounted than his fighters. Status required his horse to be unmistakably royal, but it had also to be large enough to stand out as a rallying point, and sufficiently fast to head the charge or, should the day go badly, the retreat. During many of the centuries when horses were the only efficient means of transport, the king's messengers that kept him in touch with his subjects in all parts of the realm, had to be mounted on the best and speediest animals. Those were days when, as the English bishop, Hugh Latimer, observed in 1555: 'Many horses are requisite for a king.'

Obviously the exigencies of the times and the personal preferences of different monarchs helped establish different types of horse. Richard Cœur-de-Lion and his Crusaders found their horses, the type of weight-carriers first imported by William the Conqueror, no match for the quick-turning, speedy animals Saladin and his warriors bestrode. Richard, leader of the Third Crusade and a skilled horseman, therefore encouraged his followers to acquire these fiery eastern animals for themselves and on his return from the Holy Land brought back two of his own hot-blooded 'running' horses. In the fourteenth century Richard II is said to have loved his Roan Barbary, a horse of eastern blood, like a son, but soon after Henry VIII came to the throne in 1509 any vogue for lighter horses received a setback. Chain-mail provided small protection against the deadly arrows of the crossbow, and as a young man the King imported an Italian armourer to fashion complete plate armour for him and his horse. The entire surface of this armature was covered in silver gilt and the handsome young King must have been a splendid sight, while he and his knights became more or less impervious to bowmen. But the weight, increased in the King's case by his growing bulk, needed large, heavy horses to support it. Henry ordered the elimination of as many small stallions as could be found throughout the country and imported more Great Horses from Flanders.

Henry's famous daughter, Elizabeth I, was as intrepid a horsewoman as she was a ruler, but lacked the physique to ride a large horse for any length of time. She bred war horses, to carry her crossbowmen, at the royal Tutbury and Malmesbury studs and the spirited Neopolitan coursers, popular with her nobles, at Hampton Court. But although artists of her time chose to portray the Queen riding a fiery courser of

Coronation Day, June 2 1953. The State Coach bearing the Queen and the Duke of Edinburgh passing the crowds on its way to Westminster Abbey.

state, Elizabeth was always mounted on either a Spanish Jennet, a small animal with an ambling gait, a type considered very suitable for medieval ladies, or a palfrey, a small saddle horse bred from a Jennet mare – noble looking and very gentle.

The sight of a Great Horse, the type that had carried Henry VIII's knights, is said to have bored James I 'to tears', and as the sight of a drawn sword made him feel physically ill he would not himself ride the impressive Neopolitan coursers of state, derived from Spanish Andalusians, because of their military connection. But he placed horsemanship top amongst the 'commendable' exercises a prince should cultivate, and had a passion for hawking and hunting. During his reign, light, hot-blooded horses increased in favour and continued to do so throughout the eras of the Stuarts.

By the time Charles I came to the throne, horses while remaining everyday necessities of life also increased in importance as sources of pleasure amongst the nobility. When the King rode out with his French Queen Henrietta Maria, they were often mounted on what were

The Queen at the Trooping the Colour.

scornfully alluded to by the unprogressive as 'over-valued pigmy baubles', suitable only for such fripperies as racing and hunting. Charles was an elegant horseman, accomplished in the art of the manège that was the vogue on the Continent and amongst his nobles. Early in his reign he disregarded the warning that the shortage of Great Horses in the country was affecting the supremacy of the British cavalry and that 'the French horses were in every way superior to ours'. But when war came, instead of battles with the French, it took on the hideous guise of civil war.

Due to King James's neglect and run down of his armed forces neither side started with a trained force, but the Royalists and their light horses made better cavalry material than their adversaries. Led by the dashing Prince Rupert, they were mounted on handy medium-weight animals or the 'good squat cobs' that could gallop in order to disrupt the musketeers while they were reloading. Throughout the civil war, on rough or enclosed ground pikemen on foot had the advantage, but in open country the cavalry was usually supreme.

After the defeat of the Parliamentarians at Edgehill, Cromwell, who had noted the superiority of the Royalists' horses and tactics, raised and trained his disciplined and well-mounted 'Ironsides' that were to prove invincible.

Despite Cromwell's puritanical approach to sport, said to be more political than personal, during his years as Protector of the Realm he imported more coursers and Barbs. A company trading in the Mediterranean was also instructed to look for 'good Arabian horses to furnish England with a breed of that kind'.

This policy was so successful that one of Charles II's first acts after his Restoration was to appropriate 'seven horses of Oliver Cromwell, said to be the best in England.' Charles was a fine horseman, even as a boy the pride of the Duke of Newcastle who was his eminent equestrian tutor. The Duke boasted that at the age of ten his royal pupil could ride and jump the most difficult animals and was one for whom 'horses go better than [for] any Italian or French riders'. After the ill-advised landing in Scotland that ended in defeat by Cromwell at Worcester, Charles's horsemanship stood him in good stead. Only desperate riding and various disguises during the following six weeks enabled him to reach Brighton and embark once more for France.

The next time King Charles II rode through England was on a triumphant progression from Dover to London. The crowds acclaimed everything about him including his horsemanship and later his accomplished handling of the fiery courser of state he rode to his Coronation added to the enthusiasm of his subjects.

Charles II made racing the sport of kings and established Newmarket as the headquarters of these 'running' horses and although his extravagance was a continual bone of contention, at least part of his profligacy involved importing hot-blooded horses for the royal studs, among them those 'royal mares' whose stock is believed to have helped found the Thoroughbred. Nor did the King confine his horse interests to riding. As no doubt Prince Philip is aware, Charles II encouraged the developing coach-building industry and, himself an accomplished whip, inspired his nobles to drive their own horses for sport and pleasure.

The King's niece, Queen Anne, also became a fine whip but perhaps more from necessity than choice. Her name is linked with racing, chiefly because she inaugurated the sport on Ascot Heath, but she was also accorded the title 'the mightiest huntress of her age'. When frequent though abortive efforts at child-bearing with subsequent ill health and increasing weight precluded riding, she continued to follow the Royal Buckhounds, driving a calash along grassy rides specially cut, levelled, and drained through Windsor Forest.

During Queen Anne's reign stallions from the Middle East continued to be imported, including in 1704 the Darley Arabian certified as being 'of the most esteemed race amongst Arabs both by sire and dam', a reference to the Managhi strain, and therefore considered to have the purest descent of all the Thoroughbred's founding sires.

The Elector of Hanover who became George I lacked attraction both as an individual and as a monarch. He knew little of the country whose crown he wore and cared less, spending most of his time in his native land, but at least his German outlook had a bearing on the link between crown and horses. Throughout his reign the King imported cream Hanoverian stallions with pink-tinged eyes, to be used on state occasions, a royal custom that became established and was continued until after World War I.

George II, his temper frayed by a long and tiring journey back from Hanover, fumed that: 'No English coachman could drive, no English jockey ride, nor were any English horses fit to be ridden or driven.' He also disapproved of hunting the fox, although hunting regularly with the Royal Buckhounds. During his reign the Jockey Club was set up to try and regulate what was then a distinctly irregular sport.

His grandson, the amiable if eccentric George III, did not keep a racing stable. He was an indefatigable follower of the buckhounds but not above forsaking the stag should he see a fox 'well found'. These were the times when the deer was taken to the meet by deer-cart from one of the five luxurious royal deer parks. (A forerunner of 'carted deer' hunting seen in parts of Britain between the two world wars.) Usually each animal was only required to run a few times in a season although some, like the favourites Starlight and Compton, might continue to do so for seven or eight seasons. None was intentionally injured. Occasionally, a deer became so used to hounds that it would refuse to run at all and at the end of the chase the quarry was 'taken', and then housed in comfort at some farm overnight before being returned to the deer park.

When, for a total of nine years George III was mentally incapable of reigning, his son the Prince of Wales acted as regent. As a handsome young beau his proudest boast was that he rode to Brighton and back in one day, a distance of 108 miles which took ten hours in the saddle. He was also a great man to hounds, but soon the family tendency to corpulence precluded riding and, like Queen Anne, 'Prinny' then prided himself on his expertise as a whip. Unfortunately, driving did not fulfil all his interests in horse flesh. He kept racing stables, the enormous expense of their upkeep surpassed by his gambling debts. A racing scandal, in which Prinny was in fact blameless, caused him to forswear Newmarket. His stud was sold a year later and he did not return to the turf until six years after his accession. As George IV he was driven to his Coronation in that same magnificent gold state coach in which Queen Elizabeth II was driven to hers. Ordered by George III, who used it at the opening session of Parliament in 1762, it was cited as 'the most superb and expensive of any ever built in this kingdom.'

During the reign of William of Orange, contrary to expectations, the Royal Stud at Hampton Court was kept well up to standard, and there were protests from Parliament when the horses were sold after his death. As a former sailor he had little interest in horses and it was ironic he should have met his death in a riding accident.

As her great-great-granddaughter was to do, Queen Victoria took much pleasure in her horses throughout her long reign. And although it might be hard to believe, for those who visualise Victoria as the rotund little old lady of her later years, when she was younger she showed the same liking for a good gallop as the Queen does today. She rode a great deal as a child and, according to a day's entry in the journal she was to keep all her life, her favourite pony, Rosa, '. . . went at an enormous rate; she literally *flew*. . . .' At the beginning of her reign the young Queen summoned her Master of the Horse and asked him for six chargers for her to ride to review her troops. In the habit she designed herself, dark blue with red collar and cuffs (the 'Windsor uniform' colours adopted by Prince Charles for his hunting coat), Victoria must have enchanted the regiments of Life Guards and Grenadier Guards with a squadron of the Lancers, drawn up in the Home Park at Windsor, as she cantered up and down their lines on her spirited horse. And at the big military review in Hyde Park in 1838 she was as disappointed as her troops must have been when she accepted Lord Melbourne's judgement, that it would be better and more fitting for the Queen to be driven rather than to ride for the occasion.

In the early days of her reign Victoria also delighted in showing off her dash and skill as a horsewoman in a way that the present Queen, even if she so wished, has not been able to do. This was on the frequent occasions when she led a cavalcade from the court, some thirty strong, on 'charming rides' of 20 miles or more that usually concluded with a two or three-mile gallop through Hyde Park back to the palace. The riders often included Lord Melbourne, the Queen's Prime Minister, as her chosen companion – a privilege he possibly wished he was not enjoying on the day her horse shied violently and she fell off. According to her journal the Queen was unhurt, 'only astonished and amused', although she also noted that, not surprisingly, her poor minister was 'quite frighted and turned quite pale'.

The supposedly ill effects of horse-riding on child-bearing, and her frequent pregnancies, caused Queen Victoria to ride less but did nothing to quench her love of horses. The famous Windsor Greys that draw the Queen's carriage on state occasions owe their name to the small horses, almost ponies, that her great-great-grandmother kept at Windsor for taking her around the grounds in her carriage. Some of the happiest times of Victoria's life were when she and her much loved Prince Albert and their family went north for the annual holiday at Balmoral Castle, the Scottish haven they had built on the site of an ancient and smaller castle. This was when the Queen and some of the older children were able to accompany the Prince on his shooting expeditions, riding on the broad back of Highland ponies led by gillies. These were the animals, Fyvie and the other favourites, that made Victoria feel 'so safe' as they scrambled over the rocky tracks 'never making a false step'. And as an inconsolable widow the Queen used to return to Balmoral on an annual pilgrimage in Albert's memory, riding again in the same manner to the scenes of her former happiness.

In old age Queen Victoria often took her outings in a little low-built phaeton specially constructed for her and drawn by a small pony or well turned-out donkey. It was a very different type of vehicle to the Daimler bought in 1900 by her son King Edward VII. The car heralded the era of the machine, was the first of its make to be in use as a state car for the next 40 years, and can still be seen in a small exhibition of veteran cars at Sandringham House.

The short so-called 'golden age of coaching' had begun in 1820, but by 1845 all main routes had been taken over by the railways. Three years previously Queen Victoria and Prince Albert had ventured on a journey by train, but just as this innovation failed to supersede horses in the Queen's affections, so later King Edward's motor cars had to compete with the four-legged variety of horsepower.

As the attribute of a Prince, riding had been encouraged from childhood. As Prince of Wales he hunted habitually, although not without the inevitable falls. During those times, however, fox-hunting was considered a true democratic sport and despite the dangers Edward was encouraged to participate and so 'do away a little with the *exclusive* character of shooting'.

This was very different to the attitude of horror and disapproval expressed by Queen Victoria over her daughter-in-law's wish to hunt. It was a pastime not favoured for Victorian ladies, let alone the Princess of Wales. But the lovely Alexandra from Denmark, who was Queen Elizabeth II's great-grandmother by marriage and Prince Philip's great-aunt, got her own way as usual and proved to be a brilliant rider to hounds. This was in spite of a stiff right knee, a legacy of rheumatic fever that necessitated the use of an unusual side-saddle, now in the Royal Mews, with a pommel on the off-side.

Of all sports the Prince of Wales enjoyed his racing the most. Before his accession he had a wonderful record as an owner and in 1900

The Glass Coach bearing the Queen Mother and Princess Margaret leaves Buckingham Palace on Prince Philip and Princess Elizabeth's Wedding Day, November 20 1947.

and 1910 again headed the list of winning owners. In the year in which his life ended with tragic suddenness, King Edward VII opened the season with 22 horses in training. Even on his death-bed he was happy to hear of a win by his filly, Witch of the Air, but, like Queen Victoria, Thoroughbreds were not his only love. Until ill health precluded it he rode out around his estates, Sandringham in particular, whenever he could, utilising his shooting ponies for which he had much affection.

Ponies figured prominently in the happy, boisterous childhood of Edward VII's family. Prince George, who later acceded as King George V, and his elder brother Albert Victor, began their riding careers at an early age in two panniers slung across a pony led by their horse-minded mother, the future Queen Alexandra. The second son, George, was destined for the navy and spent 15 years as a serving officer; like the sailor king, William III, he enjoyed riding although it did not become his most favoured pastime. After he became heir apparent on the death of his elder brother, he left the navy and as Prince of Wales had ceremonial duties to perform on horseback. As King he rode to take ceremonial parades and reviews. During the 1914–18 war the King's army inspections were normally carried out on foot after arriving by car but, in order to give the troops a better view of him, on his second visit to the British Expeditionary Force in France the King agreed to be mounted. Sir Douglas Haig, the Commander-in-Chief, loaned his own well-trained charger for the occasion but unfortunately, owing to a misunderstood order, the men gave such a tremendous cheer at close quarters that the mare was startled. She reared, slipped, and came down backwards, partially on her rider, who suffered two fractures of the pelvis.

King George V never equalled his father's enthusiasm for racing and owing to naval service and the war lacked the same opportunities, but he did possess a fine racing establishment at Egerton House, Newmarket. In 1925 his filly, Scuttle, won the One Thousand Guineas, making him until then the only reigning monarch to have both bred and owned a classic winner.

Like his father, King George was an expert shot and he too enjoyed riding his shooting ponies, when they carried him to and from the shoots, and on non-shooting days as well. Jock, a grey Highland that became white with age, was the firm favourite. A few riding horses and two ponies, Arabian Knight, a chestnut, and K of K, a Basuto pony given to the King by Lord Kitchener, were kept for riding in London and at Windsor, but Jock, who lived at Sandringham, became a privileged member of the royal household. He used to follow the King about like a dog, and in addition to shooting duties was the favourite mount for riding around the estate, visiting tenants and inspecting the home farm. As age and ill health restricted the King's activities, one of his remaining pleasures was to be carried round Sandringham by his 'white' pony.

When King George died in 1936 his coffin was taken from Sandringham church to Wolferton station and Jock was included in the

The Queen and Prince Philip passing schoolchildren lining the route to Royal Ascot in a horse-drawn open carriage in June 1981.

cortège, led behind the carriage carrying Queen Mary and heading the procession of the king's friends and retainers.

In 1919, when King George had decided to revive the splendid military ceremony of the Sovereign's Birthday Parade, he was attended by his eldest son, Edward, who was called David by the family. Both were on horseback, the Prince of Wales riding a length behind in the traditional position of the heir to the throne.

As small boys, David, the future uncrowned King Edward VIII, and his younger brother, Bertie, the future King George VI, were taken out riding daily by a groom. Both brothers were destined for the navy and, as a cadet at Dartmouth Royal Naval College, Bertie was encouraged to ride by a perceptive officer who felt it would help bolster the younger brother's self-confidence. The more extrovert David confined his riding activities to the holidays.

When the requirements of heir apparent necessitated the Prince of Wales leaving the service, like his great-nephew in years to come he went to university. While there, he rode to an extent during the winter, but when at home was more interested in becoming a fine shot than a first-class horseman. He himself considered his horsemanship adequate and was not pleased when the king disagreed and ordered an equerry to improve the Prince's riding. Fortunately this instructor proved to be both patient and tactful and roused his royal pupil's interest by teaching him to jump with confidence and enjoyment. A day's hunting with the South Oxfordshire Hounds then put the seal on a new pastime.

All four of the King's sons became very popular with the hunting fraternity of the fashionable packs they supported. Prince Albert, conscientious in all he undertook, had become the best rider, but the Prince of Wales found few thrills to equal that of galloping and jumping a good horse on a line of his own. Soon he was combining his hunting with racing, competing in point-to-points and finding both sports provided the means of proving his courage and endurance on equal terms with others.

As Prince Charles knows very well few can hunt in this intrepid manner without a quota of falls, and as he has also discovered like his great-uncle, these can be nothing when compared with those one can take when racing. Charles II took part in races as a 'gentleman jockey', but Edward was the first heir apparent to ride in a race. The King and Queen were watching when he won at the Household Brigade meeting at Hawthorn Hill and were naturally very proud. They were also apprehensive about the dangers attached to this sport, a feeling shared by many of their subjects. When a bad fall in a point-to-point in 1924 resulted in concussion and a month in bed for the Prince of Wales, the public outcry was such that both the King and the Prime Minister begged him to give up the sport. But Edward did not comply until four years later, at the urgent request of his mother when the King was recovering from an illness.

In view of the strong feelings expressed by the 'antis' of today it may seem curious that no-one had the smallest objection, on any grounds, to the Prince of Wales continuing his fox-hunting, but as all his hunters were potential 'chasers they were sold and he no longer rode to hounds.

During the last six years of King George V's reign, despite the small assortment of royal cars, the state horses were still frequently used for everyday transport as well as on ceremonial occasions. When the new King Edward VIII presented himself to the customary Accession Privy Council in London the day after his father's death, he flew in from Sandringham in his own plane. He was the first British monarch ever to fly and was the creator of the King's (Queen's) Flight. Although at various times when Prince of Wales he played polo, tried the hazardous sport of pig-sticking in India, and took carriage horses and vehicles on the royal train during the extensive and incredible tour of that continent, there were occasions when his royal regard for horses wore a little thin. There was the space and the necessity for horses on the 4000-acre ranch the Prince bought in Canada. In South Africa, in search of exercise and as a relief from boredom he sometimes abandoned the royal train to gallop into town with the welcoming posse of Boer farmers. But there were moments during his protracted world tours when the popular Prince of Wales could well have dispensed with the horse-drawn transport thought fitting for the occasion.

As King, Edward was essentially a man of his progressive, changing era. By the time he acceded he preferred to relax by playing golf

A view from the crowd of the procession for the State Opening of Parliament.

or gardening rather than riding a horse. Had protocol allowed he would have liked to walk short distances rather than travel in the immense Daimler that was the symbol of 'the King passing by on his business'. No doubt he would have been happy to go down in history as Edward the Innovator. During his reign that only lasted 352 days between accession and abdication, he in some ways showed little regard for tradition and a poor understanding of the obligations of monarchy, yet this King had no wish to be remembered as Edward the Reformer. It was an outlook that was extended to the state horses. When Edward VIII went to his first and only State Opening of Parliament by car, it was the weather rather than his wishes that kept the carriage horses standing in their stalls in the Royal Mews.

Chapter Two

The Work of the Royal Mews

THE GATE porter on duty at the entrance to the Royal Mews today is required to enforce rules that differ little from those issued in 1785 to his predecessor in charge of the gateway to the royal stables. They were: 'To suffer no loose, idle or suspicious persons, or women of the town to lurk or harbour near the Mews and to shut the gate at ten at night.'

King's Mews existed in the reign of Richard II, but in those times their function had nothing to do with horses. A mews, the name derived from the old French *mue* (from the Latin *mutare* – to change) was a building where the King's falcons were kept during their 'mewing' or moult. For centuries the monarch's birds were housed in mews near Charing Cross, but when Henry VIII's stables situated in what is now Bloomsbury were burned down, the King decreed that his hawks should be replaced by his horses.

When George III bought Buckingham House from the Duke of Buckingham in 1762 the stabling there was used in addition to that at Charing Cross. The present attractive and constantly used Riding House (School) was completed four years later. Then in 1824, four years after George IV came to the throne, he commissioned John Nash to redesign the stables and coach houses. Nash was the same famous architect commissioned to make massive alterations to the house, a lavish conversion that took so long the 'New Palace in St James's Park' was not quite completed by the time Queen Victoria came to the throne. The stabling, however, became the Royal Mews in 1825, the date shown on the weathercock above the handsome porch.

The entrance to the Royal Mews is from Buckingham Palace Road under a Doric archway. The complex is designed as a quadrangle, the eastern side still housing the state coaches, the west and north quarters still providing some of the finest stabling in existence. There are more coach houses behind the quadrangle. These are used as garages for the royal cars: the five official Rolls Royces, the youngest and most important being the Phantom VI given to the Queen in 1978 as a Silver Jubilee presentation; the two Austin Princess limousines and the luggage brakes. The Vauxhall brake and Rover saloon the Queen drives herself are also kept there, with Prince Philip's Range Rover and, when he is in London, Prince Charles's 1970 convertible Aston Martin or his Range Rover.

The King's Coachmen busy cleaning semi-state harness in the Royal Mews.

A view inside the stables of the Royal Mews at Buckingham Palace.

The Royal Mews in London is the headquarters of the Royal Mews Department that includes the private mews at Windsor Castle and Hampton Court Palace, and that in Scotland when the Queen is in residence at the Palace of Holyroodhouse in Edinburgh. It is a very busy and far-reaching department, responsible for the personnel, the priceless historic contents of all the mews, the royal cars, the Queen's horses, with the exception of the Thoroughbred stud and racehorses, and a great deal more besides.

Originally, the Royal Mews came under the direct supervision of the Master of the Horse, an office ranking next to those of Lord Steward and Lord Chamberlain and one of great honour and antiquity, with records of every appointment since 1391. In Roman history there are references to the *comes stabuli*, the horse thegn or staller of the Teutonic chiefs, and after the Norman Conquest the royal horses, kept mostly for war and distributed amongst the king's manors, were in the overall charge of the *Custodes Equorum Regis* (the Keepers of the King's Horses). In 1783 the responsibilities were extended to include the King's Buckhounds, the royal pack that was abolished when Edward VII came to the throne.

The 10th Duke of Beaufort, the Queen's Master of the Horse who retired in 1978, was originally appointed in 1936 by Edward VIII

Final preparations are made on the Glass Coach before setting off to take Lady Diana to St Paul's on Royal Wedding Day, July 1981.

and held office longer than any of his predecessors, serving three sovereigns with great distinction. He has been succeeded by the 15th Earl of Westmorland – an accomplished horseman who rode in the first three-day event at Badminton – whose forebear held the same office to George III.

The first Crown Equerry, the name derived from *écurie* meaning stable, was appointed in 1854 as secretary to the Master of the Horse and superintendent of the Royal Mews, but five years later the two appointments became separate. Subsequently, the Master of the Horse, while remaining the third great officer of the court and personal attendant to the sovereign on all occasions involving horses, ceased to have executive command over the mews. The department was then renamed the Royal Mews Department and came under the jurisdiction of the Crown Equerry who, as he does today, then acted as the executive officer to the Master of the Horse.

Charles II had eleven equerries who attended him in turn, their duties mostly involving horses. One was for an equerry always to ride in the leading coach, presumably to draw the fire of any would-be assassin. When he was not actually waiting on the sovereign the job included the 'mouthing, managing (manègeing) and breaking the saddle horses, and preparing them for the King's riding.' When the King travelled, equerries

rode on horseback beside his carriage, a practice continued into the early part of King George VI's reign. Another of the original duties was to hold the King's stirrup while he mounted his horse, a requirement that led to some dilemmas for any equerry attending the unpredictable George III. It was 'the King's delight to mount his horse before the equerry in waiting could possibly be aware of it; often in severe and unpleasant weather which rarely deterred him, always at an early hour'. One unfortunate equerry 'when thus surprised has been compelled to follow the King down Windsor Hill with scarcely time to pull up his stockings under his boots.'

Happily, the present Crown Equerry is unlikely to be involved in any such eccentric proceedings. He does sometimes attend the Queen when she is riding round her estates, and is in attendance when she mounts her horse in the inner quadrangle at the palace before riding out, side-saddle, to take the salute at the Trooping the Colour.

The wide responsibilities of the Royal Mews Department today mean that Lieutenant Colonel Sir John Miller, KCVO, DSO, MC, who has held office since 1961, is a very busy man. Apart from running his department he is responsible for all ceremonial occasions that involve horses. The outstanding quality and precision of the processions on Prince Charles's wedding day were due to Sir John's meticulous planning and rehearsing. As Crown Equerry, the man in overall charge on all such occasions, he is driven, in a car, at the rear of the cortège ready to deal with any of those hitches that have to date been mercifully conspicuous by their infrequency.

To the uninitiated, the Royal Mews, with its priceless collection of coaches and carriages, the historic sets of harness, the gifts of magnificent saddlery presented through the centuries from rulers in so many parts of the world, may seem to be just a museum, an attractive anachronism, whereas in fact, it is a busy, working stable that is also a kind of centre of equestrian life in London. Many horsemen, would-be and actual, come there seeking help and advice. Thousands of people flock in on the two afternoons a week the mews are open to the public, to see the treasures, admire the trappings of the past, all of which are usable, many still in use today, and become acquainted in the flesh with the carriage horses the majority only see on television.

The Royal Riding School, where the Queen practises riding side-saddle in the weeks before the Trooping the Colour, is so booked up that care is now needed to save damage to the floor from so many hundreds of hooves trampling the surface throughout the year. This is where the carriage horses are schooled under saddle and by means of a record-player receive their initiation into the horse-scaring sounds of military bands and cheering crowds. The mounted police often use the school, and a room is set aside for the use of those connected with the Coaching Club, Animal Welfare, and the London Van Horse Parade. Each week during term-time GLC schoolchildren ride there, and four separate groups of the Riding for the Disabled Association come weekly

Coronation Day, June 1953. A final inspection of the grooms who walk each side of the postillions, shown with the crooked sticks which they use to keep an even pull on the traces.

to carry on their splendid work inside the safe enclosure of the walls. There are frequent lectures and demonstrations in the riding school, and occasionally such eye-catching events as a pageant of different breeds for the benefit of some visiting VIP.

To work in the mews is no sinecure – work with horses seldom is. Horses, carriages and stabling have to be kept in extra immaculate condition. As for 'tack'-cleaning, those sets of ancient, irreplaceable state harness can each just about be oiled and polished in time for the job to be started again. But there is pride in the work, the atmosphere is happy, the modernised flats above the coach houses where the married men live are both convenient and comfortable, and the working conditions are good – a point emphasised by the excellent long-service record amongst the staff. The Queen's wheel postillion on that royal wedding day, formerly a sergeant in the Grenadier Guards, has a son also working in the mews. The coachman who drove Queen Elizabeth the Queen Mother has been in royal service since 1955; the Prince of Wales's lead postillion both to and from St Paul's, who also drove the Prince and his bride to Waterloo Station, has now retired after 49 years of royal service; the wheel postillion, with 26 years to his credit, is following in the steps of his father-in-law and grandfather-in-law, both royal coachmen. The coachman who had the honour of driving the bride and her father in the glass coach to St Paul's had at the time 22 years in the royal service to his credit. In 1982 there were two fathers with sons working in the Royal Mews and five or six sets of brothers.

Even in this electronic age there are always a number of young men applying for work in the mews. Most of those who are accepted can already ride, but driving is almost always an unknown art that has to be taught. Obviously one of the attractions of the job is the lure of a future that could include the expertise and great responsibilities that go with wearing the black, semi-state or full-state liveries of a royal coachman or postillion. To be seen in such a position on ceremonial occasions, wearing the magnificent traditional garments of historic interest that are symbolic of the prestige of the Queen's service, is obviously a heady goal. In the years between the possibility and the attainment there are the undoubted attractions, for those who like them, of working with horses.

The horses housed in the Royal Mews are the carriage horses, the teams of the famous Windsor Greys, always used to draw the Queen's carriages but only brought to live in London after the death of King George V, and the other twenty or so bays. In the past, with the exception of chestnut, almost every colour of horse has been used for the sovereign's state occasions. Those notable creams imported by George I continued to be bred at Hampton Court and used for occasions of the highest state until in-breeding and the impossibility of replacements precluded them in the first quarter of this century. They were succeeded by the black stallions, in turn supplanted two years later by the bays.

The Windsor Greys are a specific colour and one that lightens with age, but not a specific breed. Like the bay horses they are mostly half-breds, some of English or Irish origin, one Hungarian, but predominantly Oldenburgers. Hanoverian horses continued to be imported for royal use until well into the present century and others were brought in from France, Spain, Morocco, and Holland. Until recent years, the majority were still being bought abroad, mostly from Denmark, Holland, Germany, or Sweden. It was not a deliberate policy of by-passing British breeds but finding a number of suitable, matched horses in Britain is mostly a matter of luck involving much time and travel, whereas there are more well-organised studs of non-thoroughbred horses to be found on the Continent.

Some years ago a number of very good Oldenburg mares, some bay, some grey, were bought in from West Germany. Due to the nature of their work and the high standard of horsemastership in the mews the royal horses are normally in use to a ripe old age, but it seemed wasteful

A display of Coaches which are housed in the Royal Mews. Left to right: the Balmoral Sociable, the French Charabanc, the Irish State Coach and two State Landaus.

Coronation Day, June 1953.
The State Coach postillions.

not to breed from some of these animals. The idea appealed to the Queen, partly because she has always been interested in breeding horses, and from time to time there has been a 'home bred' amongst the carriage horses, but principally because it seemed a sensible and more economical policy. To save expense she has now closed her small stud farm at Old Windsor, but the Royal Paddocks at Hampton Court, the palace built by Cardinal Wolsey and ceded by him to Henry VIII, are again in use for the traditional purpose of breeding carriage horses. Stock is bred from the Oldenburgers, now all retired as brood mares, and from any other suitable mares in the mews.

For many decades some of the inhabitants of the Royal Mews have been Cleveland Bays, a breed that originated as sturdy pack ponies but were bred up with Thoroughbred blood to become the Yorkshire Coach Horse, popular in Edwardian times and very similar to the modern Cleveland. Until his death in 1981 the Queen owned a well known Cleveland Bay stallion called Mulgrave Supreme. Bought in the early sixties to save him from being sold abroad, the horse, a fine example of what was then almost an extinct breed, was broken to both saddle and harness at Windsor and showed promise as a jumper. He was then loaned out to become a most successful sire of half-bred hunters and was instrumental in re-establishing the only British breed of coach horse.

The Queen's harness mares are bred to outside stallions, often to Cleveland Bays, and since the majority of stallions of this breed are descendants of Mulgrave Supreme, some of the present state horses carry his blood, so that purchase of twenty or so years ago has paid a good dividend.

For the lighter, faster work demanded of the royal carriage horses today, half-breds are more suitable than the slower, heavier pure-bred Clevelands. Most of the royal horses are now home bred, the younger ones out of predominantly Dutch mares, the older ones out of predominantly Oldenburg mares. The Cleveland Bay–Oldenburg cross is an interesting one that is closely linked, with both breeds possessing Thoroughbred blood and an inter-cross. Originally, the Oldenburg was evolved with a percentage of Andalusian and oriental blood, but like the Cleveland has been bred up with Thoroughbred blood and also with the use of some Cleveland Bay sires.

The Queen is a true horse-lover but she does not subscribe to Bishop Latimer's sixteenth-century contention regarding a king's (or queen's) need of many horses – not unless they serve a practical purpose. In recent years, despite the increase in various horse activities in which some members of her family take part, she has been cutting down on numbers and the finances are strictly controlled with any extravagance cut out. This policy is shared by all members of the royal family. Nowadays, many of the riding horses are handed down in much the same way some families hand down clothes. Purple Star, for instance, Princess Anne's first event horse, now in his twenties, has been taken over by Prince Edward. In 1982 the Princess, still competing in three-day events at the highest levels, had only one 'top' horse in event-training, with two or three young ones being brought on. Prince Charles, riding with hunts in which the first flight may well keep half a dozen hunters, makes do with two, occasionally three horses.

The majority of the royal coach horses are dual purpose. Those who watched the royal wedding on television may have noticed Prince Philip, on arrival back at the palace with the bride's mother, Mrs Shand Kidd, pausing to speak to the driver of their state landau and pat the pair of horses. This was Prince Philip's own coachman, 'the chap who sits at the back' when the Prince is competing in driving events; the horses were two of the mares from the team he drives.

For more than a decade now many of those beautifully turned-out horses seen on ceremonial occasions trotting sedately down the Mall, oblivious alike to the cheering crowds, the bands, and banners, are also driven, not quite so decorously, along rough country tracks, through the initially fearsome novelty of river fords and between obstacles of a kind never encountered on London streets. This is the sport Prince Philip

A fine view of the State Coach bearing Queen Elizabeth II passing Eros on Coronation Day.

adopted when he gave up playing polo and thought of utilising horses and facilities already to hand in the Royal Mews. Competitive driving of four-in-hands (and of singles and pairs of both horses and ponies) is now a national and international sport and for a number of years the royal horse teams, the bays driven by Prince Philip, the Windsor Greys by the Crown Equerry, have been carrying the flag for Britain both at home and overseas, competing always with distinction and often with success.

Rio, a grey Oldenburg gelding named to commemorate the Queen's 1968 state visit to Brazil, is at 18 the eldest of her highly trained teams of greys. In his competing capacity he has been to Poland and twice each to Hungary, West Germany, and Switzerland. On state duties, which needless to say take precedence, Rio and his team-mates have accompanied the Queen to Berlin and to many other parts of Europe.

Like the horses that draw them, the majority of the coaches and carriages housed in the Royal Mews are in use. Each vehicle has its own historic past, each is in working order, and a shining example of the beauty and practicability of the coach-builder's art. Perhaps it would be difficult to imagine the Queen and her family and guests setting off for a picnic at Balmoral in the French charabanc, an amazingly roomy vehicle with an awning top, driven from Paris to Windsor in 1844 as a gift for Queen Victoria from Louis Philippe of France, but it is still drivable. It seems a pity today's traffic and roads prevent the Queen from sharing the same enjoyment her great-great-grandmother obtained from the state sledge. According to Queen Victoria's journal it 'went delightfully . . . the horses with their handsome red harness and many bells [having] a charming effect' when Prince Albert drove her on the snowy roads around Brighton.

Pride of place in the mews has to be given to George III's 24-foot long, 4-ton gold state coach, with its fantastic embellishments of symbolic palm trees, pineapples, lions' heads, cherubs and other figures, the sides, back and front adorned with panels painted by the Florentine artist, Cipriani. The coach has been used for every Coronation since that of George IV and, except during Queen Victoria's reign was generally used by the sovereign for the State Opening of Parliament. Since World War II it has only twice been on the road, once for the Queen's Coronation and again in 1977, when she and Prince Philip were driven to St Paul's Cathedral for her Silver Jubilee thanksgiving service. The coach, overhauled a number of times and regilded for that occasion, needs eight horses to pull it. Until World War I they were always the cream stallions, but in 1921 and 1922 the black stallions were substituted. Bay horses were then used until the Coronation of King George VI when the greys were first employed. The horses are postillion ridden and, since the coach can only proceed at walking pace, there is a liveried groom walking, for extra control, either side of each pair of horses. Originally, the horses wore the blue state harness, made for George III and used until after Queen Victoria's accession, that is still in the mews today. Today's number one set of red morocco state harness used only for the

ABOVE: *The gold State Coach used for the Coronation since George IV.*

LEFT: *Detail from one of the panels on the side of the coach painted by the Florentine artist, Cipriani.*

RIGHT: *Close-up of one of the superb gilt figures adorning the coach.*

gold coach, is richly embellished with gilt ormolu, the other seven sets equally ornamented in brass. Number three is generally used with the Queen's state carriage. All eight were made in 1834, but reserved for the next six years until Queen Victoria and Prince Albert decided to utilise a set when going to dine with the Lord Mayor of London.

Each of these sets of harness weighs about 110 pounds and this, combined with the impracticability of altering such ancient leather to fit different horses, has caused the occasional problem. For some years the leaders of the royal teams, unlike the wheelers, were driven without the bearing reins that, loosely fitted, still help to keep the heavy bridles in place. But this was remedied after one of the Windsor Greys, part of a team en route to Edinburgh station to meet the Queen, lunged its head down and the cumbrous bridle slipped over its ears leaving it in an embarrassing and potentially dangerous state of undress. More recently, the Crown Equerry retained his normal equanimity when the ancient bit in the mouth of one of the leaders suddenly parted, during a progression of royal horses and carriages round the mews for the benefit of the television cameras.

Amongst the sets of harness in everyday use for the different types of carriage are treasures now unused, such as the unique set ornamented with goose quills. The superb pony harness, together with a miniature pair-horse driving landau presented to the Queen's father and his brothers and sister when they were children by the Showmen of England, has been used since with a pair of New Forest ponies, and two Caspian stallions, the oldest known breed of horse or pony.

All the coaches and carriages reflect the workmanship of times when things were made to last, and do credit to the care they have received since. Broughams built before or at the beginning of the century are still driven twice daily carrying official messengers around London. The remaining town coach, known as King Edward VII's town coach and stored at Windsor during World War II, is one of the two vehicles sent to convey a new ambassador when he goes to Buckingham Palace to present his credentials to the Queen. It also carries the serjeants-at-arms, their long golden maces protruding from the windows, to and from the State Opening of Parliament. And on those occasions it is driven behind Queen Alexandra's state coach, another also used regularly for conveying ambassadors, that carries the imperial state crown ahead of the Queen's procession to and from Parliament. This coach, originally a 'plain town coach' built about 1865, was converted into a 'glass state coach' for use by the then Prince and Princess of Wales when they went to big social occasions such as the opera, balls, and concerts. Later, King Edward VII used it for state dinners and levees, and on his death it was transferred to Marlborough House for Queen Alexandra.

When, weather permitting, the Queen and Prince Philip drive to the Royal Ascot race meeting to start each day with that traditional and colourful procession up the course, a custom instituted by George VI, they use one of the five Ascot landaus that are also employed for official visits but normally kept at Windsor Castle. These elegant carriages, smaller and lighter than the semi-state landaus, have basket-work sides and are pulled by postillion-controlled horses. Sometimes, where space is restricted, there may be only a pair of horses but for the splendours of Ascot there are always four Windsor Greys, the postillions wearing state livery in the Queen's racing colours – as they did for Prince Charles on his wedding day.

On that day the Prince was driven to St Paul's in the splendid 1902 state postillion landau with four grey horses and Lady Diana and her father arrived from Clarence House in the glass coach. With its specially large windows this coach, bought before King George V's Coronation, gives a good view of the occupants and has a happy association with royal weddings. It was used by the Queen when, as Princess Elizabeth, she married Prince Philip, an example since followed by Princess Alexandra and Mr Ogilvie, and Princess Anne and Captain Phillips. Generally, the glass coach also conveys the bride and bridegroom away from the church, but the new Prince and Princess of Wales headed their carriage procession back to the palace in the open state postillion landau that gave the crowds a splendidly uninterrupted view of them.

On that day all eight state landaus, the oldest made in 1838, were used in the processions. The Queen, with Prince Philip on the way to St Paul's, and accompanied by Earl Spencer in the procession after-wards, was using one of the semi-state postillion landaus, that was Queen Victoria's favourite type of carriage on ceremonial occasions. One has been utilised by the Queen in recent times for historic occasions, such as her Coronation visit to Edinburgh, the Investiture of the Prince of Wales at Caernarvon, and the Silver Jubilee visits to Glasgow and Cardiff.

The Queen has a great admiration for her great-great-grand-mother and part of her love of Balmoral stems from the unmistakable impact of Queen Victoria that still permeates the castle. When she looks at the old Queen's 'own dear Scotch Sociable', usually known as the Balmoral Sociable, she must be aware of the same aura. The carriage, upholstered in the Balmoral tartan, was used regularly by King George V to go to Crathie Church and to the Braemar Gathering, and is a master-piece of durable workmanship. Amongst other intrepid expeditions, Queen Victoria took it to Switzerland where she was 'driven straight up into the splendid mountains' to spend 'a miserably cold and cheerless night' at an hotel 8000 feet up. The carriage bears a plaque: 'Lucerne St Gothard Pass Furca Rhone Glacier Engelberg Aug. & Sept. 1868' to record the fact. Victoria's courage, another characteristic that appeals to the Queen, is illustrated by the entry in her journal made a week later, where the route is described as '. . . an unpleasant, *nervous* road, so rough and narrow . . .'. Parts of it were also alluded to as being precipitous, a way one would suppose scarcely suitable for a royal carriage and four, even if the horses and driver were Swiss.

Occasionally, instead of the Sociable, Queen Victoria rode her pony Flora on an excursion, and here again the Queen has a link with the Victorian past. Her racing interests and expertise in the complicated field of Thoroughbred blood lines are well known, but her abiding love of horses is not confined to the aristocrats of the horse world. The Queen's affection extends to 'the animal on four legs' irrespective of size or breeding, and this includes the small number of ponies bred and worked at Balmoral. Predictably, pride of place is given to the Highlands, the sturdy, placid breed, for centuries the crofters' 'jack of all trades', like Queen Victoria's Flora and other ponies. They are larger than the Fells, introduced soon after World War I, but these ponies, once used to carry 16 stones of lead across the fells to the sea and sometimes covering 240 miles a week, are equally strong. Some of those at Balmoral today have blood-lines going back to the ponies ridden by King George V in the twenties. He used to keep one in London to ride in Rotten Row and in 1977 the Queen had a colt foal out of a Fell mare that was a direct descendant of those ridden by her grandfather 50 years before.

The Queen also breeds Haflinger ponies at Balmoral, descendants of two mares presented to her during her state visit to Austria in 1969. They come of a sure-footed mountain breed, perhaps the most useful of all Austrian work horses, and although smaller than the Highlands or Fells are also very sturdy weight carriers. In their native country they are adept at bringing the hay crop down the steep mountain slopes on sledges. In winter, with coloured harness and silver bells setting off their attractive chestnut coats with cream manes and tails, Haflingers are in demand at the fashionable ski-ing centres for providing sleigh rides.

Some Highlands and Fells have always been bred at Balmoral and now, as with the Haflingers, the Queen's policy of home breeding is firmly established. Her Highland stallion, Balmoral Fafernie, and others of the breed have done well in shows and helped bring these useful ponies to the fore, and all three breeds are kept as working animals. After being sent south to Windsor to be broken to saddle and harness, they return to the estate as dual or treble workers in return for their keep.

When the royal family are in Scotland for their annual summer holiday they sometimes combine pleasure with petrol-saving measures by using the ponies for driving out onto the hill. Prince Philip drives a pair of Fells or Haflingers, sometimes a four-in-hand of Fells, to compete in local driving events. From 1982, in early summer when the grounds are open to the public, all the suitable ponies are being used, driven in pairs to a specially designed cart for taking visitors on tours of the estate.

The shooting and deer ponies are still employed at Balmoral as they once were on all the big estates before the advent of the ubiquitous Land Rover, for bringing home the day's bag of grouse in panniers, or toting the carcass of a culled stag.

During the stalking season two or three of the ponies are kept close by the different Balmoral deer forests, large areas of wild moorland, ready for the pony-man to ride or drive one of them to some spot adjoining the site of the day's sport. Once there, he tethers the pony and uses his telescope to watch for a thread of smoke on the horizon. This is the signal that one of the number of stags destined to be culled during the season has been shot with a rifle, by a stalker who will have spent many hours demonstrating supreme endurance and skill in order to achieve his goal. The pony-man then replaces the pony's riding or driving tack with a headcollar with bit and lead-rope, girths up the heavy deer-saddle with its webbing breeching for extra support, and sets off leading it on his long trek across the rough terrain. Once loaded with the 14 or 15-stone carcass the pony carries it back to the track, to be collected later by Land Rover. At the end of the day the pony is either driven home, or sent on its own back off the hill, on an unattached journey that presents no problems.

Autumn through to spring is the busiest time for the deer ponies, when the gillies cull the hinds. Just as it is important to control the number of stags, so this is necessary in order to keep the herds of wild red deer healthy and within bounds, so that their numbers remain in correct ratio to their feeding grounds and they do not become a menace to farmers.

The coachman and footmen in state livery stand before the Glass Coach on the Prince and Princess of Wales' Wedding Day, July 1981.

Chapter Three

Queen Elizabeth: Her Riding Career

THE QUEEN was born into a horse-loving family. When she was a young child her father, then Duke of York, hunted regularly until he disposed of his hunters in the cause of economy. Her mother rode as a girl, her interest in horses blossoming after the accession into the ownership of steeplechasers, a hobby the Queen Mother still enjoys to the full. The King always counted riding as his favourite means of relaxation, although the war years and then increasing ill health sadly limited the time he had to indulge it. But as soon as Elizabeth, and later Margaret too, were old enough and sufficiently expert it was a mutual delight to go riding in Windsor Park with their father.

After the move to Buckingham Palace when Elizabeth was 10 years old, horses, from the mounted police on duty outside the palace controlling the crowds gathered for the Changing of the Guard, to the squadrons of the King's Life Guard (now the Queen's Life Guard) clattering past on their way to and from Whitehall, were part of the everyday scene. There were the times when the children could watch the processions of horse-drawn carriages leaving the palace on some ceremonial occasion. It was a treat to be taken by the Queen in a barouche and pair, to Horseguards Parade to watch the King take the salute at the Trooping the Colour. From babyhood, Elizabeth had been taken along to the Royal Mews to see and pat the royal carriage horses in their stables. When she was three she was given a rotund little Shetland called Peggy, the first of the much loved ponies that were to share her and Margaret's childhood.

Some people tend to imagine that because a horse or pony belongs to the royal family or is ridden by one of its members, it must be a paragon of breeding, looks and behaviour, but this is very seldom the case. Those ponies the Queen rode as a child were much the same sort of animals that other children ride, and certainly none of them was pricey. One quite large pony is recorded as having cost 45 guineas – not exactly a vast sum even in those days.

The Queen has remarked that a number of her horses in the past have not been quite what she would have chosen for herself. She had them because they were gifts, and when she was quite young the pony, George, came into the same category. The King and Queen had been visiting a Durham coalmine, and had stopped to look at a small Shetland pony type that was about to go down the pit. Within minutes George had been

Princess Elizabeth and her favourite pony, Greylight, on her thirteenth birthday.

presented to them, a gift for the young princesses. He arrived straight from the pithead, mane and top of the tail shaved in the manner required for his work and his wayward character doing little to offset his odd appearance. There was Gem, the typical thick-necked, hard-mouthed little pony that graces, or disgraces, so many homes and Snowball, a 13.2 cob bought out of an Irish jaunting car and with sufficient charm to offset a tendency to whirl in circles when required to move on.

Queen Elizabeth riding side-saddle on Burmese.

One or two of those ponies of the Queen's childhood made small mark, even fewer are remembered as a bad joke. But whatever they did or did not do they are recalled with affection, although until the advent of the Welsh Mountain, Greylight, none could have been described as the perfect pony for a child to ride. Greylight, however, had manners to match her looks, and it was a sad day when, by the time Elizabeth was 12, both she and Margaret had outgrown the little mare.

Greylight was then given to the late Mr Horace Smith, the owner of well known riding stables in Cadogan Lane, who with his equally well known daughter Sybil undertook the princesses' riding instruction for a time. Twice a week during the early summer of 1938 the Smiths brought two of their own ponies to the riding school in the mews, and these lessons, that included jumping, supplemented the princesses' basic riding and horse-sense learned from the family groom. By the end of the following summer Britain was at war.

The royal family had been holidaying as usual at Balmoral and when war was declared the King decided that his daughters should stay on in Scotland in the care of their governess until Christmas. They had a couple of ponies to ride and drive and since many of the royal staff had been called up the princesses had the new pleasure of looking after Jock, a bronze-coloured deer pony, and the smaller Hans, a Norwegian, largely by themselves.

The Queen always likes to delve below the surface of anything in which she is interested. When she was a child her ponies had been brought out, groomed and tacked up ready for her to mount, but the riding had never been the end of the matter for Elizabeth. She had gleaned everything she could from grooms and instructors about a pony's welfare and management, and those months in Scotland with Jock provided the golden opportunity for getting to the heart of the matter. There is a photograph of this pony taken at Windsor many years later with an inscription on the back in the Queen's handwriting: 'Jock – who taught me more than any other horse', but what she learned did not only concern looking after him. On that score the pony is partly responsible for what is very evident when the Queen is looking at or handling a horse – that she knows her subject. But Jock can also take some credit for the Queen being such a good, natural horsewoman. His antecedents are unknown but something considerably more fiery than pure Highland blood went into that pony's make-up. He was viceless, but a lively animal, quick in his reactions, one that really had to be ridden, and he provided Elizabeth with the same kind of mutual fun and rapport enjoyed by all those who form a good relationship with horse or pony.

During the later part of the war the princesses went intermittently for further instruction to the Smiths's stables, then at Holyport near Windsor, and during this time, at the suggestion of Horace Smith, Princess Elizabeth was given a little insight into the art of riding side-saddle. Horses had by then superseded the childhood ponies and a variety of animals were adding to Elizabeth's experience. Even as a child her specialised educational requirements as heir to the throne prevented her riding as much as most pony-minded children, or as much as she would have liked. This applied even more as she grew up and her public commitments increased, but riding and horse interests were firmly established to become, as they have remained, the Queen's most enjoyable form of relaxation.

Amongst the horses of those early years was Trustful, a little mare much enjoyed by Elizabeth as a riding horse, that had been handed down by her cousin, the tall Princess Alexandra who found the mare too small for hunting. Another, Trim Ann, who came from Lavinia, Duchess of Norfolk, was looked after at Windsor and ridden frequently by Alexandra before going to the Sandringham stud. As a brood mare, Trim Ann then became the dam of many notable royal horses of the future, including Columbus.

Many people find it difficult to imagine the Queen and Prince Philip leading an ordinary kind of home life or indulging such everyday occupations as drinking a cup of tea. Much the same dilemma governs some of the public's conception of the Queen's private riding, imagining her confining her horse to the occasional dignified trot, but nothing could be further from the truth. The Queen has said she leaves the finer nuances of modern equitation to Anne, but she is herself an excellent natural rider. She has a great rapport with her horses and they always go well for her, and she enjoys a good gallop as much as her great-great-grandmother. Like the rest of her family the Queen could be described as a bit of a speed-merchant, whether on a horse or driving herself in a car. Once, at Balmoral, the privileged writer waiting to follow on after the royal family when they drove off for a picnic, with the Queen at the wheel of the leading Range Rover, had cause to remember a royal chauffeur's warning that she would be lucky if she could keep up!

So much of the Queen's life is spent in a blaze of publicity and under the relentless, probing eyes of television and press cameras that some absorbing form of relaxation is a necessity. This is what riding provides for her, but not only in the enjoyable form of hacking out. She has always taken a great interest in schooling some of the favourites and the good manners of her horses, both past and present, owe a great deal to the training she has herself given them. There have, however, been exceptions and the aptly named Surprise, a grey North African Barb, given to her by Lord Louis Mountbatten when she was in Malta with Prince Philip before the accession, according to his owner remained 'a diabolical ride' to the end of his life. This did not detract at all from the Queen's enjoyment when she rode Surprise, like Queen Victoria she appreciates horses that 'give her something to do', and his speed was exhilarating. He was fun to ride in that early morning scamper up the straight at Ascot that was inaugurated by the Queen a long while ago for the enjoyment of her family and guests, and is now usually headed by Princess Anne and one of her event horses.

The majority of the Queen's riding horses are long lived, still

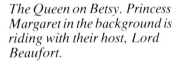

The Queen on Betsy. Princess Margaret in the background is riding with their host, Lord Beaufort.

working happily and full of life when in their early twenties and so they remain good companions for many years. Betsy was a classic example, bought by the Queen from a local farmer in 1953. She was a black/brown mare whose character and performance made up for what she lacked in blue blood. She quickly established herself as the favourite and dominant personality amongst the riding horses and remained so until, in honourable old age she was retired to the royal paddocks at Hampton Court. Rather to her racing manager's surprise the Queen then wanted to breed a foal from her favourite, but Betsy settled the matter for herself by refusing to have anything to do with the idea!

Betsy was one of the few horses the Queen bought for herself. Nowadays the two she rides, both originally intended for polo, are home bred. In the years when there were many more horses in the Windsor Mews than there are today the majority had been presented to the Queen by other heads of state. A horse is the obvious gift for someone known to be as knowledgeable and interested as the Queen, but it is an offering that can present problems.

Sultan was not one of them. A Thoroughbred bay gelding, bred in Pakistan but descended from two Derby winners, he was presented by the President of Pakistan in 1959. Very good looking and an exciting ride, Sultan became co-favourite with Betsy and continued in that capacity for many years. But sometimes the gift came from a country that considered that nothing less than a stallion would be sufficiently prestigious, and it was not always easy to find a suitable role in the Windsor Mews for an entire of some exotic breed.

Melekush, a stallion of the very fast and ancient Akhal-Teke breed, was given to Prince Philip by Marshal Bulganin and Mr Krushchev when they visited Britain in 1956. The horse proved useless at stud but, contrary to expectations, lived quite happily with the mares and geldings in the stables. He did not bite as such, but as a stallion it was natural to him to take hold of things with his teeth. When out on a ride, if he was allowed to stand on a loose rein and happened to latch onto someone's arm or leg or horse, it tended to cause a certain amount of excitement. Otherwise, except for pulling a bit due to keenness, the Russian horse was well mannered and a good ride. Until polo and its practice fully occupied the Prince's leisure time he occasionally hacked Melekush out on family rides, but the horse was ridden principally by the stud groom. Despite being what is essentially a desert breed the horse was a good jumper and was eventually loaned to a lady rider who competed with him quite successfully at Riding Club level.

Zaman, a golden dun of the Russian Karabakh breed, arrived at the same time as Melekush, as a present for Prince Charles. The little stallion proved his worth at stud and, before going to stud in Wiltshire where he remained, sired Cossack that was out of an English Thoroughbred mare and became one of the Queen's riding horses. When Princess Anne remarked enigmatically that Cossack 'could be very Russian!', no doubt she had in mind his suspicious nature, ability to evade being caught, and a total and successful aversion to having his head clipped, but the Queen rode him with enjoyment for many years. Now, quietened by age, Cossack is retired to the royal stud at Polhampton, where he acts as a reliable 'nannie' to the young Thoroughbred stock.

There were many questions about a suitable role for Bussaco, another stallion that was given to the Queen in 1957 by the Portuguese President. But despite the curious scything action of a Lusitano bred and trained for the Portuguese form of bull-fighting, the horse was so comfortable to ride, so sweet natured and well schooled, that both the Queen and Princess Anne rode him occasionally and he became very popular with the Queen's guests. Bussaco sired a colt foal out of Pampera, one of the Crown Equerry's polo ponies, and eventually went on loan to a stud in Gloucestershire where he remained to the end of his life. The foal, aptly named Oporto, was sold as a young horse and developed into quite a promising eventer.

Pride, a small desert Arabian now retired to act as 'nannie' at the Sandringham stud, was a gift to the Queen from King Hussein of Jordan in 1958. He too arrived as a stallion but was later gelded. In his many years at Windsor he was sometimes ridden by the Queen and frequently by Princess Anne who used him as a second string to her pony, High Jinks. Pride was a lively, co-operative ride, with a playful 'spookiness' that was fun but demanded his rider's full attention.

In these days the only gift horse amongst the riding animals in the Windsor Mews is Reneau, a North African Barb, presented some years ago to Prince Philip by the late President Boumédienne of Algeria. Of the same breed as Surprise but even better looking, Reneau is exceptionally well mannered (unlike his predecessor) and a general favourite. This was the horse the Queen chose to ride all afternoon in the pouring rain during driving trials at Balmoral in 1981, and he is especially liked by Prince Edward. Another that the Prince enjoys is Flame Gun – like Purple Star once Princess Anne's eventer but precluded from the sport by injury and passed on to her youngest brother for less strenuous forms of riding.

In the years before the numbers were being cut down, some of the Queen's ex-racehorses were occasionally sent to Windsor to end their days as hacks. One of these, Agreement, was the well known winner of the Doncaster Cup and, twice, of the Chester Vase. When he 'broke down' the Queen refused to put him to hurdling, but success on the racecourse seldom makes for a good hack. In his youth and before being gelded Agreement had been something of a 'rogue' and was so wild no-one could do anything with him. At Windsor he proved very lazy, and at first, because he had always been one of a racing string, it was impossible to get him out of the stable yard by himself. Even when these and other troubles were overcome by patient schooling, out on a ride Agreement would idle along grinding his teeth and then suddenly demonstrate a burst of his racing speed, before applying four-wheel brakes as he caught up with the leading horse in the party. He always appeared uninterested in what he was doing and the Queen, who was very fond of her ex-racehorse, thought he looked rather sad. But although she consented to use him during a photographic session, she wisely decided against any action shots! In the end, Agreement reformed and became Princess Margaret's favourite riding horse.

Royal Worcester was another that came off the racecourse to become a hack. Bred by the Queen at Sandringham, the big bay became the property of the Marquess of Abergavenny and was put into training as a 'chaser. When the horse refused to race he was returned to the Queen Mother and eventually arrived at Windsor. There, used principally for riding by the Queen's guests or by the grooms, Royal Worcester was a success, despite retaining his penchant for carefree, and unseating 'cat-leaping' (a partiality for jumping five-bar gates that exist only in the horse's imagination!).

Queen Elizabeth attending the third day of the annual horse trials at Badminton in 1959.

At the time of the Queen's Silver Jubilee there were three ex-racehorses in the Windsor Mews: Castle Yard, one of the Queen's well known winners on the flat, Queen Elizabeth's ex-steeplechaser, Master Daniel, and the French-bred horse, Worcran. To prove the exceptions that make the rules, all three became good riding horses and were used regularly as general hacks, the first two also ridden from time to time by the Queen, and Worcran habitually by Princess Margaret. Another that was frequently the Queen's choice then and for some years was Bellboy, sired by Le Bel, at one time a stallion standing at Sandringham, and out of Trim Ann – parentage that made Bellboy a half-brother to Columbus, and the eldest of that famous 'family'.

Nowadays, with the Queen's financial policies in mind, neither sentiment nor convenience is allowed to sanction the appearance of another horse in the Windsor Mews unless there is a useful niche for it to fill. The Queen herself now has only two horses kept exclusively for her own riding. Both were bred for polo, and were in fact played, and both are by College Green, the smaller of her two Thoroughbred stallions that stand at the Wolferton stud in Norfolk. Amongst other successful progeny, College Green sired Queen Elizabeth's good 'chaser, Queen's College.

One of these royal hacks is Courtyard, a chestnut mare with a lot of white about her, whose dam was the polo pony, Gussie's Love, belonging to the late Archie David, and was one of the brilliant, often Argentine-bred ponies for which he was famed. Greenshield, the Queen's other horse, at one time a polo pony for Prince Charles, should certainly satisfy his owner's taste for speed. Also sired by College Green, his dam, Betaway, was a Thoroughbred granddaughter of the 1933 Derby winner, Hyperion, and was probably the fastest polo pony Prince Philip ever rode. Before retiring to stud in the early sixties, Betaway became something of a legend with public and players alike. It used to amuse Princess Anne to watch out each season for the inevitable press headline about her father: '. . . flying down the polo ground on this pony bred from Derby winners!' Once, when the Prince asked a famous high-goal player why he gave up racing against him for the ball, his adversary remarked: 'Well, when I saw what you were riding I knew it was no good!' The Prince used to say that riding Betaway on the straight was like riding a powerful motor-bike – open the throttle and away she went, and maybe Greenshield gives the Queen the same exhilarating feeling of acceleration.

When the Queen takes the salute on Horseguard's Parade at the splendid military ceremony, Trooping the Colour, it is the only time when, wearing the attractive adapted uniform of Colonel-in-Chief of one of the Guard's Regiments, she rides side-saddle. This is the day, usually in the first half of June, when the Household Division pays tribute to the sovereign. From the time the Queen rides out from the palace into the roars of cheering that create an almost tangible atmosphere, to when, the parade over, she wheels her horse at the palace gates to face the march past of the Old and New Guards, the entire proceeding is the epitome of

The Queen comforts Burmese after the dramatic events at the Trooping the Colour ceremony in June 1981.

Princess Elizabeth showing her command of side-saddle riding in 1947 at the first Trooping the Colour since the War.

meticulous, smooth-running military precision. But few will forget the ugly incident that marred the Trooping in 1981.

On that occasion, a youth living out a 'fantasy' assassination that was so nearly 'for real', fired blank shots at the Queen as she wheeled her horse round the narrow entrance from the Mall to Horseguards Parade. Her mare leaped forward. Although inured to the mounted police 'nuisance training' that includes gunfire, she was probably more startled by the sudden rush of police and troops behind her than by the shots. She was quickly controlled and calmed by the Queen who, displaying the same self-possessed courage she was to show a year later when awoken by a strange man pulling her bedroom curtains, continued with the parade as though nothing had happened. But even though those shots were blanks (and at the youth's trial it appeared that live ammunition might well have been used), with a less skilled horsewoman there could have been a serious accident, and one can only be thankful for a very sensible decision taken way back in 1947.

That was the year when King George VI revived the ceremony of his official birthday parade and decided that, as heir presumptive,

The Queen, Prince Philip and Prince Charles at the Trooping the Colour ceremony.

Princess Elizabeth should accompany him. He felt it only fitting she should ride side-saddle at the Trooping the Colour, and the late Mrs Archer-Houblon, an expert in the art, was asked to instruct the Princess. At the time there were those who felt it would be quite sufficient if the Princess could sit correctly at the walk, but her instructor wisely insisted that her able and co-operative pupil must be secure and capable at all paces, and under most forseeable circumstances.

The first time the Princess accompanied the King, riding half a length behind him in the traditional position of the heir to the throne, she was mounted on a hunter called Tommy that belonged to the Duchess of Beaufort, brought to London and trained for the job by Mrs Archer-Houblon. The next year the King was not well enough to ride and Princess Elizabeth rode beside his carriage on Winston, the police horse that had been her father's mount on the previous occasion.

This big chestnut, a handsome horse with exactly the right looks and temperament for a military ceremony, then carried her with distinction each year until he had to be put down after slipping up in the street five years after the Queen's accession. Winston became very well known to the public and his successor, another chestnut called Imperial, received the same public interest and attention during the many years he carried the Queen to the Trooping. Occasionally, if Imperial was lame (he was eventually put down owing to foot trouble), the Queen rode one or another of the horses the mounted police kept in reserve for such a contingency. In fact, her choice of horse was never stated until the evening before the Trooping, and in the few weeks before the parade when the Queen always practises her side-saddle riding in the school in the London Mews, she often rode one of the 'possibles' while Mrs Archer-Houblon worked Imperial. Once or twice on the day, the honour of substituting for Imperial fell to Doctor, an endearing little grey, once to a comparatively young horse called Neil. One year, when the unbelievable happened and Imperial and both understudies were lame, the lot fell to Fairway.

This was a sober old character of no great looks that normally acted as charger for the late Duke of Gloucester at the Trooping, and was noted for the comfortable straddle with which he evened out his rider's weight when they were halted. In those days the Duke usually rode with Prince Philip in attendance on the Queen, their horses each side of hers and the requisite distance behind. During the long halt on the saluting base it seemed that Fairway felt he should be on equal terms and on station with the Queen's horse, and it always amused her to watch the unobtrusive shuffle with which he tried to remedy the situation. But on that never-to-be-forgotten day when Fairway himself carried the Queen he never moved a muscle throughout the long ceremony. He was out in front where he had always considered he had the right to be.

Since 1969 the Queen has ridden Burmese to the Trooping, the black mare concerned in the 1981 incident, that was presented to her by the Royal Canadian Mounted Police. Burmese was bred at Fort Walsh in

The Queen riding Burmese at the Trooping the Colour in the uniform of Colonel-in-Chief of the Irish Guards. Behind her, Prince Charles, Major H. P. D. Massey (Field Officer) and the Earl of Westmorland (Master of Horse).

Canada, and already beautifully trained, proved impeccable on parade. She is also such a pleasant and mannered ride, partly due to the Queen's further schooling, that she spends part of the year in the stables at the Windsor Mews, including the few weeks before the Trooping the Colour, when Sir John Miller's niece, Sylvia Stanier, reaccustoms her to ceremonial duties and to carrying a side-saddle. For the remainder of the year Burmese is kept in the Hyde Park Metropolitan Police stables, at work on street patrol, escort and other duties of an ordinary police horse.

In the early seventies, another black horse, a young one, was presented to the Queen by the Mounties at Regina during one of her Canadian tours, and was then handed over at Windsor seven years later during her Silver Jubilee celebrations. This is the 17-hand Centenial, first ridden by Prince Charles behind the gold coach when the Queen and Prince Philip went to St Paul's for the thanksgiving Jubilee service, and since then on several occasions at the Trooping the Colour. Otherwise, although Centenial is the Queen's horse, he is kept in the mounted police stables in Old Scotland Yard and worked on the same duties as his stable-mates.

In 1982 when Mr Reagan became the first President of the United States to visit Britain and he and Mrs Reagan stayed at Windsor Castle, he expressed the hope that he could go riding with the Queen. As she is very proud of her two Canadian-bred horses, the Queen decided they should have the honour. She gave her distinguished guest the handsome Centenial, using the smaller Burmese for herself, and Prince Philip drove Mrs Reagan in a carriage-and-four behind the riders as they toured the Home Park. On this occasion the President, a keen and experienced horseman, declined the offer of a Western saddle to which he is more accustomed, and chose to ride with an English saddle.

For some while, the Metropolitan Police supplied horses for members of the royal family and some chiefs of staff to ride at the Queen's Birthday Parade, but this practice has been discontinued for many years now and the family ride their own horses. The Queen of course rides Burmese, Prince Philip uses one of his own horses, and Prince Charles has the Queen's Centenial. In recent years, the mount of the Master of the Horse has been either one from the Royal Mews or Banner, a great character belonging to the Queen that acts as an outrider's horse on all ceremonial occasions and is otherwise on loan to the police. The Crown Equerry usually rides a horse with an interesting history that is also the property of the Queen. This is the good-looking Bachelor Gay, now 23 years old, that in his youth won the Ladies Side-Saddle Championship at Dublin. Like Banner he is also loaned to the police and, fit and well, is still happily engaged helping to train police recruits at Imber Court, the mounted force's training establishment at East Molesey.

The Queen gets great pleasure from her horses whatever their particular role may be, but she is entitled to take most pride from having become, entirely by her own efforts, one of the world's acknowledged experts in the very complex field of Thoroughbred blood-lines.

The Queen, riding Burmese, and her guest, American President Ronald Reagan, on Centenial, set off on their hour long ride in Windsor Home Park in June 1982.

Mr Reagan was the first American President to be a guest of a British monarch since 1918.

Chapter Four

Royal Bloodstock

RACING IS often known as the 'sport of kings', but interest in horseracing and all that it involves is not an exclusively male prerogative. The 'sport of monarchs' might be a more accurate tag.

Queen Anne ran horses at York and instigated a race for Her Majesty's Gold Cup, that was run off in heats and in which her own horse, Pepper, came third. At the time England, basking in Marlborough's victories against the French, was taking little interest in any sport, and showed small enthusiasm when the Queen drove from Windsor Castle with her courtiers to attend a day's horseracing organised at her command. But Queen Anne's name has lived on in the racing world, because those enjoyable races run on a day in 1711 took place on Ascot Common, where the famous racecourse was laid out under her orders.

Queen Victoria was not interested in racing as such but she was happily and successfully involved with breeding Thoroughbred yearlings for sale. She kept twice the number of royal mares there are today, and during her reign seven classic winners were bred at Hampton Court, then the royal stud, amongst them the famous filly, La Flèche, winner of the One Thousand Guineas, the Oaks, and the St Leger.

The royal studs were founded at Hampton Court in the sixteenth century, making the Royal Paddocks probably the oldest stud in continuous existence in the world, but during the eighteenth century they were based mainly in Windsor Great Park. Here, they were under the auspices of the Duke of Cumberland, the second son of George II, who was the first member of the royal family to be elected to the Jockey Club. Before his death, the Duke had revived interest in racing at Ascot, but his chief claim to racing fame lay with the two great stallions produced at the royal studs during those years. King Herod was eight times champion sire, and four fifths of all modern Thoroughbreds are descended from the great unbeaten Eclipse.

Today the royal stud farms are at Sandringham, the principal stud, and at Wolferton, each of which houses a stallion. The Queen also leases a stud at Polhampton, not far from Windsor.

The entrance to the Sandringham stud is dominated by the great bronze statue of Persimmon, the almost legendary winner of the 1896 Derby and other classics, that belonged to the future King Edward

The Queen and the Manager of the Royal Studs at Sandringham, Mr Michael Oswald, admire her Classic winning filly, Highclere.

The Queen and Prince Philip riding in an Ascot Landau in the sunshine at the races.

VII. He was a great patron of the turf and, as Prince of Wales, established his own studs at Sandringham and Wolferton, in the last quarter of the eighteenth century, in addition to Hampton Court where they were centred from the reign of George IV. As King he also owned Diamond Jubilee, a full brother of Persimmon, that despite an uncertain temperament won its royal owner the racing accolade of the Triple Crown, that is the Two Thousand Guineas, the Derby, and the St Leger – in the same year that his horse Ambush II won the Grand National. In 1909, the year before he died, Edward VII won the Derby for the third time with the leased Minoru, a horse of special interest to the Queen because it figures in the ancestry of the great stallion Aureole that was left to her by her father.

The reigns of both King George V and King George VI were disrupted by war, and fortune did not often smile on the royal studs throughout the nineteen-twenties and thirties. During this period, however, the two great foundation mares, Feola and St Therese were bought, that were to have a profound effect on the future. By the forties four of their high-class daughters were successfully changing the royal racing scene, first on the racecourse but principally as brood mares. One of these, Angelola out of Feola, was Aureole's dam, while his sire Hyperion was the small chestnut great-grandson of Minoru that won the 1933 Derby – and ran on half way round the course again before he could be pulled up.

The King died before Aureole's racing career began, but when he left his daughter this horse, potentially an immensely valuable animal at stud, he knew that Elizabeth's interest in Thoroughbreds and racing already extended beyond the thrills and disappointments of the race-course. During the war the King had leased horses from the National Stud, that came into being during World War I when Colonel Hall-Walker (later Lord Wavertree) gave his very good Irish-based stud, comprising stallions, brood mares, yearlings, and foals, to the nation. During World War II the land and buildings were sold to the Irish government and all the stock shifted to England where the stud was re-established at Gillingham in Dorset and West Grinstead in Sussex, and run under the auspices of the Ministry of Agriculture. In those days the policy was to breed and sell the produce they did not want. Anything they thought they might like to keep was leased to the King for racing, later to be returned to the stud.

The King began leasing these horses in about 1941, and Big Game and Sun Chariot were two of the first, and most famous. They and his other National Stud horses were trained by the late Fred Darling at Beckhampton, and the King and his family used to stop off to take a look at them when en route to stay at Badminton House. Princess Elizabeth, already a devoted horse-lover, was fascinated with the whole set-up of a trainer's yard, but the attraction was not confined to the horses and their work-outs. She wanted to know how they were bred and why, and picked Fred Darling's brains on the intricate topic of Thoroughbred blood-lines. Little did he know it was a subject his questioner would one day make her own, to become an acknowledged world expert.

Aureole was two when the Queen acceded and, in his early racing days particularly, provided her with plenty of interest and

LEFT: *Princess Elizabeth pats Monaveen after a magnificent win in the Queen Elizabeth Steeplechase at Hurst Park in December 1949.*

RIGHT: *The Queen with her Ascot winner Aureole in 1954.*

excitement as well as some disappointments. The colt's temperament did not make him an easy ride and even Eph Smith, the jockey who got on best with him, had some dodgy moments when Aureole boiled up, over-excited by the noise and commotion of the crowds. There were a number of spectacular bouts of plunging and rearing before the start of races and occasionally one had the feeling that the royal chestnut was not going to participate at all. Even as a more mature four-year-old, in 1954, it looked as though the Queen's horse would not be in the line-up for the prestigious King George VI and Queen Elizabeth Stakes, in which he had come second to Pinza the year before. After playing up in front of the stands, Smith had wisely taken Aureole out of the parade. He was then taking the colt direct to the starting gate when his mount took an unseating aversion to the raising of a spectator's umbrella and deposited his jockey on the track. The obvious next move for a highly strung Thoroughbred colt would be to gallop off into the distance, but Aureole was always unpredictable. He began grazing as placidly as any old pony, and then allowed himself to be caught and remounted. It was as well the horse decided to co-operate that day as he then went on to win this 1½ mile race.

Good as Aureole was (or could be) it was unfortunate for the Queen that the horse most likely, to date, to win the Derby for her should in 1953 have come up against the spectacular giant, Pinza, that beat Aureole into second place. However, he won her seven races, including the Coronation Cup and Hardwick Stakes, was placed four times, materially contributing to her heading the list of winning owners in 1953.

At stud, Aureole had his revenge on Pinza, for the big horse

Doutelle after winning the 2000 Guineas Trial Stakes at Kempton Park in 1957. The Queen, Princess Margaret, her trainer Captain Boyd Rochfort and her racing manager, Captain C. Moore, look on with delight.

was a racing success that proved of little worth as a sire. The Queen's horse was leading sire in 1960 and 1961 and second in 1965. By 1972 he had sired the winners of 500 races in all parts of the world and he only retired from stud in 1974.

Aureole, now dead, used to stand at Wolferton, like Sandringham a private stud in Edward VII's day. In succeeding reigns the breeding activities were gradually transferred from Sandringham and the paddocks were partially closed down for about thirty years, the resident stallion being housed at Wolferton. Sandringham was re-opened in 1959 for Doutelle, a descendant of the priceless Feola line and the winner of seven races for the Queen. Tragically, the horse died towards the end of 1962 as the result of an accident in his box. He had only completed four seasons as a sire but already his progeny were proving their worth and his future as an influence on the world's bloodstock seemed very bright.

Not only from this point of view was the stallion's demise a terrible blow to the Queen, but it was also the loss of an animal she knew and cared for as a personality. She has the same personal feeling for all her bloodstock – racehorses, brood mares, breeding stallions, yearlings, and foals – that she has for her riding horses and the ponies at Balmoral. The Queen also combines a wonderful 'eye for a horse' with a photographic memory, a gift that has often been put to good use. During her Commonwealth tour of Australia in 1977 she visited the Lindsay Park stud in the south and was shown the very successful stallion, Without Fear. To everyone's amazement, the Queen said she remembered the horse well, having seen him as a foal during a private tour of the studs in Normandy ten years before. The Queen's memory for horses was also needed when Doutelle first arrived. He came with Agreement, another chestnut colt, and in some way their labels had been lost and it was difficult to decide which was which. But the Queen had originally 'picked' Doutelle as a foal and had no trouble in recognising him again.

One of Doutelle's progeny was Canisbay, whose successful dam, Stroma, had been selected by the Queen from the 1956 Doncaster St Leger Yearling Sales catalogue, and bought for a very modest 1500 guineas. By winning the Eclipse Stakes, Canisbay ended the royal studs' five-year run of little success on the racecourse. He then stood as a stallion at Sandringham, for some of the time that Colonist II was there, Sir Winston Churchill's doughty ex-chaser whose progeny, in different capacities, have been very evident amongst horses of the royal family. Another link with Doutelle that must please the Queen, is that Bustino, the syndicated stallion now resident at the Wolferton stud, is one of Doutelle's grandsons.

Each year after Christmas the royal family's holiday at Sandringham gives the Queen an enjoyable opportunity to see life at her royal stud at first hand. Apart from the few days in April when she usually manages to come and stay on the estate to see the season's crop of foals, those weeks in January are amongst the comparatively few occasions when the day-to-day happenings at the stud can be seen and discussed on the spot.

Both Sandringham and Wolferton have been public studs since the late fifties, in the sense that both the resident stallions are syndicated. The Queen is a major shareholder in each horse and amongst other shareholders Lord Halifax has an important interest in Shirley Heights, standing at Sandringham, and Lady Beaverbrook in Bustino that she herself bought in 1972.

The bay Bustino, foaled in 1971, was the winner of five races and is the Epsom Derby course record holder. By 1981 he was the leader of his generation of sires and, reckoned to have made more rapid advance than any other stallion in Britain, seems set to become firmly established as one of the strongest factors in high-class breeding.

The younger horse, Shirley Heights, is the winner of six races, including the 1978 Derby, and Irish Sweeps Derby, that earned him the title 'Horse of the Year'. He is rated the best son to date of the incomparable little Mill Reef, a horse that was invincible at 1½ miles and won 12 of his 14 races, including the 1971 Derby and a year later the French plum, the Prix de l'Arc de Triomphe. In 1972 Mill Reef shattered his foreleg when at exercise. The injury was so bad it was possible he might not be able to go to stud, but veterinary brilliance combined with the little horse's co-operative disposition helped him become 90 per cent sound. Mill Reef stands at the National Stud and Shirley Heights, in addition to inheriting much of his sire's racing ability and breeding potential, has also the same lovely temperament.

During those weeks at Sandringham the Queen has the opportunity to become acquainted with a few of her 30 or so brood mares, those that are going to the home stallions or the one or two that may be foaling too late to be covered that year. But in an industry that takes in other people's work at the most important time of the year, the Queen mostly sees the 90 to 100 visiting mares. These come in from all parts of the world to foal at the studs before being mated, usually in the proportion of half each, to either Bustino or Shirley Heights. At the same time the royal mares will be at other studs, also in many parts of the world, having their own foals and then being mated with the stallions the Queen has decided are most suitable.

Each year, when the mating programmes for the royal mares are drawn up, the Queen discusses the various options with Lord Porchester, a life-long friend of the royal family who is her racing manager, and Mr Oswald, her stud manager. At these sessions both men put forward their own ideas, but most originate with the Queen, the acknowledged expert and inspiration in this and other stud affairs. Lord Porchester and Michael Oswald have shared the overall responsibility for the Queen's bloodstock since 1970, but her advice and comments on all stud matters are so sound that her stud manager, who regularly reports the day's happenings back to the Queen, usually by telephone, says he looks on himself more as the under-manager to the Queen's management.

The Queen with Lester Piggott at Goodwood Race Course in 1964.

The Queen, Prince Philip and the Queen Mother looking over the field at the Epsom Derby.

The objective of all Thoroughbred studs is to get the visiting mares in foal and then, with their current foals at foot, send them back home by the end of July at the latest, repeating the process in the following season that each year begins in January. The second half of the year is much quieter, and that is when the staffs at Sandringham and Wolferton (with both studs run on identical lines) concentrate on the royal mares that have been returning throughout May, June, and July. They also have the most important work of looking after and weaning the foals in preparation for sending them to Polhampton in November.

This stud is used partially for resting horses out of training, or the odd one injured during training or that has proved a bit backward and needs more time to mature. Fillies in need of being freshened up also go to Polhampton, but the stud is primarily devoted to the care of the yearlings that stay there until ready to go into training some 10 or 11 months later. The stud is under the supervision of Lord Porchester who lives near by and is also quite close to Kingsclere and West Ilsley where the Queen's trainers, Ian Balding and Dick Hern operate. The West Ilsley stud was bought by the Queen in 1982. As the same vet who attends Sandringham also serves Polhampton there is the continuity right through that is so essential. And since all three establishments are within easy reach of Windsor, when the Queen has time she can keep in touch with her young stock, and with some of those in training.

The Queen usually has an average of 20 horses in training each year, about half with Dick Hern and the remainder divided between Ian Balding and William Hastings-Bass. During the flat-racing season she is in daily touch by telephone with her trainers. There is always a great deal to discuss, principally deciding on the most suitable race for a particular horse at that stage in its racing career, dependent on its breeding, and the level it has reached in training and fitness. After the exciting day when a horse wins, its future can usually be assessed with a little more certainty. The disappointments, more common to all owners than the successes, have to be considered in the spheres of cause and effect.

Officially there is no specific 'royal' jockey although, since the Queen has second retainer on Willie Carson, at the time of writing he really comes into that category. It means that if Major Hern, who has first retainer on him does not require Carson for one of the Hern stable horses, then, if required, he rides for the Queen. Failing Carson, Lord Porchester in conjunction with the trainer concerned would find another jockey. It could well be Lester Piggott or Joe Mercer who have both frequently worn the royal colours, or perhaps the American jockey Steve Cauthen, Wallie Swinburn, or Edward Hide who all do so from time to time.

Unless some unexpected public duty of first importance should make it impossible, the Queen always goes to the Derby where, in common with every owner of high-class bloodstock, she hopes one Derby day to be cheering her own three-year-old past the winning post to gain the Blue Riband of the Turf.

The traditional date in mid-June for the royal meeting at Ascot, is another the Queen and Prince Philip try to keep clear of other engagements, and much of the historical pageantry and elegance of Ascot would be lost without the royal procession instigated by George IV in 1825, of five open landaus which drive up the course before the racing each afternoon. Most years the Queen manages to attend the King George VI and Queen Elizabeth Stakes and in a good year may have the bonus of the Epsom spring meeting or perhaps a day at Kempton or Newbury. Even if there is the possibility of getting to watch one of her horses run, an excitement enhanced because the animal is usually the creation of her own decisions, it is never easy to organise because of the many 'imponderables' that can affect a horse. The fixture may be made well in advance, but it is impossible to know until two or three days beforehand whether the animal is actually going to run. When it comes to the point, therefore, the Queen sees what she can of her horses racing, when she can – and that is not very often. Given the opportunity she may be able to watch them on television, and nowadays video tapes make it possible to 'capture' a race for later consumption. In common with the yearling sales, attending race meetings to study the form is a 'must' for an owner, but these are the occasions when Lord Porchester and Mr Oswald are able to act as the Queen's eyes and ears.

As for winners, the royal studs, like most, have had seasons of

Australia Fair, a two-year-old racehorse presented to the Queen by the Australian Government, arriving at the Newmarket Stables of William Hastings-Bass.

exciting success, and periods of disappointments. When the Queen first came to the throne she carried on her father's tradition of leasing horses from the National Stud, an enterprise that was of course entirely separate from the royal studs. One of these, a filly called Carozza, captured the Oaks for the Queen. Hopeful Venture, sired by Aureole and another success she leased from the National Stud, was the last stallion bred there and the last of the horses to be leased. The stud changed its policy in the early sixties when it was moved to Newmarket and it was decided to give up breeding and concentrate entirely on stallions, either bought in or occasionally given by generous owners. The object was to prevent high-class horses, those which private enterprise could not afford to keep,

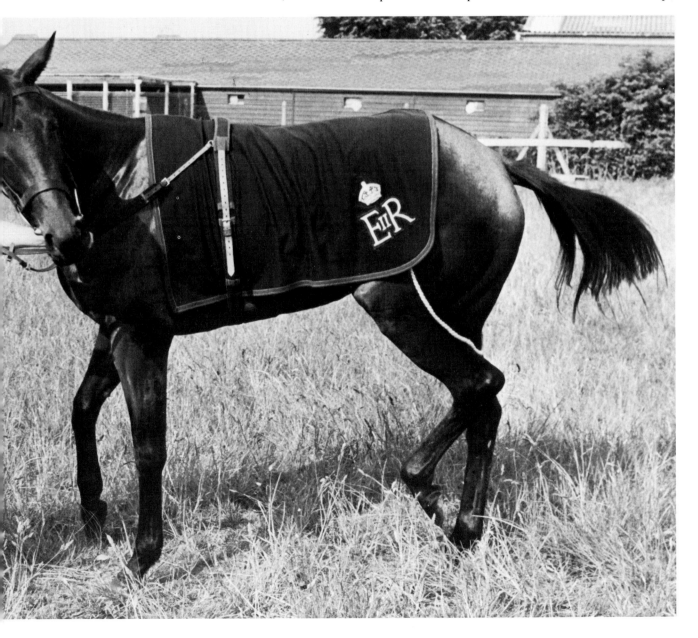

from being sold abroad and is a policy that has proved very successful. Many famous horses of famous and invaluable blood-lines have stood, or still stand, at the national Stud and from time to time the Queen has used all the present seven residents for her mares.

During the 1970s the royal studs were on the crest of the wave comparable to the first years after the accession, and they have since remained there. Dunfermline, now a valuable asset to the stud as a brood mare and perhaps the best racehorse the Queen has bred to date, won the Oaks in the Silver Jubilee year of 1977 and went on to a great win in the St Leger. Highclere, a notable character who is the star mare in the stud today, won the One Thousand Guineas and the French equivalent of the Oaks, the Prix de Diane, when the Queen who was at Chantilly to watch her, was given a great reception by the wildly enthusiastic French crowd. Highclere holds the record amount of money won in one year by a filly trained in England. Another of the best fillies racing for the Queen in those years was Example, who won the Park Hill at Doncaster and two big races in France. Sadly, she came to a tragic end, dying after foaling for the first time.

In 1982 one of the Queen's best two-year-olds was St Boniface, a very promising colt that was a winner at Newmarket, and one considered to have a bright future – at that stage no-one was mentioning the 1983 Derby, but a winner there for the Queen is obviously the prime goal.

In the same year the Queen won the Lupe Stakes at Goodwood and the Prince of Wales's Stakes at Newmarket with Height of Fashion, another very good filly whose dam is Highclere. The filly was then sold to Sheik Hamdam al Maktoum, one of the many Arab owners now encouraging the long-term future of British racing by a willingness to expend a great deal of money on the high-class fillies they lack.

By such a purchase, the Arabs are enjoying an entry into the sport that concerns Thoroughbreds, the breed built on the descendants of three imported Arabian stallions.

To have sold a filly like this, bred by herself of the famous Feola line and successful on the racecourse, must have been a wrench for the Queen. But she is eminently practical and always aware of the difficult financial times in which we live. The horses of the royal studs are the Queen's private property, and although breeding and racing Thoroughbreds is a vastly expensive business, sales like that of Height of Fashion in many seasons enables the royal racing account to pay for itself.

Today, racing and breeding are increasingly becoming big international business and the royal studs form a relatively small operation. Their fortunes, however, should continue to flourish and exert influence on the world's bloodstock breeding, because quality is the vital ingredient – and quality is what the Queen's horses possess.

Chapter Five

Prince Philip: Polo Enthusiast

PRINCE PHILIP says he cannot remember when he first learned to ride and now, with more than sixty years of jam-packed life behind him, that is scarcely surprising. There is, however, a photograph of him aged 9 or 10 riding with his cousin Michael of Roumania beside the Black Sea near Constanza. His expression is a little grim, but whether that was due to the proximity of his horse or to that of the photographer it would be hard to say. At Gordonstoun he was instructed by Dr and Mrs Saloschin. It is alleged that he began riding 'under orders' from his headmaster, Kurt Hahn, for laughing at others who enjoyed a horse interest he did not at that time share. As was to be expected at that practical-minded school, like all the boys who rode Philip was taught stable management and had to help look after the ponies. Unlike the Queen, however, whatever riding Prince Philip did in his youth was not likely to have been more than as a spasmodic pastime, and his childhood was not spiced with any lengthy involvement with the joys and indignities that go with ponies.

After leaving Gordonstoun the Prince entered Dartmouth Royal Naval College as a cadet in May 1939, only a few weeks before he was 18 and not many months before the outbreak of war. He left Dartmouth in 1940 and was then on active service with the navy until the end of the war. In all, Philip spent 12 years in the navy, until he was granted indefinite leave in July 1951, never since rescinded. That was when the King was so ill that Princess Elizabeth and Prince Philip took on more and more of his public duties. In those years there was little time and few opportunities for activities with horses except for polo, started after the Second World War under the auspices of his late uncle, then Lord Louis Mountbatten. At the time Philip was First Lieutenant in HMS *Chequers*, a flotilla leader in the Mediterranean fleet and based in Malta. Lord Louis, author, as Marco, of one of the best books on polo ever written, was building up naval polo again after the war years and his nephew proved a keen participator. When Princess Elizabeth came out to Malta to join him she enjoyed watching him playing polo, even if in those early days he was possibly showing more enthusiasm than skill.

After the King's death and the Queen's accession in 1952, as Prince Philip has said, '. . . the whole thing changed very, very considerably . . .'. His life as a serving officer was behind him, and although his priority has always been to help and back up the Queen in every possible

Prince Philip capturing the ball during a polo match at Cowdray Park in July 1967.

way, he was also carving out a job for himself in a situation in which there was no precedent. His success is illustrated by the innumerable interests with which he has been and still is involved to the common good, but it was not always easy. Anyone whose life is spent mainly in the public eye knows the sheer necessity for some absorbing form of relaxation, and the Queen well understood her husband's need for violent exercise to keep him physically fit. Playing polo fitted the bill admirably, and he played as often as he could from the start of the season, in those days at the end of March, to its end in mid-August.

The attributes of a natural player are courage, coolness, an aptitude for ball games that includes a 'good eye', team spirit, and adequate horsemanship. The lucky possessor of all these desirable qualities, Prince Philip also has the determination to make a success of whatever he undertakes. Polo handicaps range from minus two, the lowest, up to ten goals, a level only achieved by a very few players. Always a '200 per center' in anything on which he embarks, be it work or play, the Prince quickly developed into a hard-hitting, forceful player of high-goal polo. For many seasons, whenever he could spare the time, he played with the Windsor Park team, and at his peak had the satisfaction of having his handicap raised to five goals. Despite the damaged wrist that reinforced his decision to give up polo when he was 50, his handicap did not drop below four goals, which is well above the average standard.

Prince Philip says that even if he was not now 'old and decrepit' (his own words, that scarcely fit the facts!) finances would no longer allow him to play polo. At the same time he makes the valid point that high-goal polo is no more expensive than some other sports, such

1964. Prince Philip and Prince Charles practising together on Smith's Lawn near Windsor Castle.

as motor-racing or competitive sailing, practised at comparative levels.

Prince Philip's yard in the mews at Windsor is small and compact, the tack and work rooms at one end, the food stores at the other and with 10 loose boxes in between. Nowadays, this is where he keeps his driving team when they are not required in London, consisting usually of five horses and never more than six. In the polo-playing days the Prince's ponies were housed in the yard, the clatter of their hooves as they were ridden out during the season combining with that of the Queen's riding horses, and that of the numerous Household Brigade Polo Club ponies that then inhabited one of the courts in the mews.

The majority of Philip's ponies were Argentine bred. They arrived already schooled but by slightly different methods to those employed in England, and done mostly on a loose rein. This results in the ponies carrying their heads lower than their English counterparts and turning quickly by a kind of shuffle of their front legs, whereas the English animals are taught to swing round on their hocks. Basically, all polo ponies are schooled to what Prince Philip considers to be the elements of dressage comprising the disciplines, obedience, and skills required of any well trained horse or pony whether ridden or driven. He illustrates the point with the story of one of his brothers-in-law, a first-class horseman who was selected for the German Olympic three-day event team just before the war. The Prince was still playing polo when this brother-in-law came to stay at Windsor Castle and Philip offered him a ride on one of his polo ponies called Nijinski, a splendid animal from the Argentine schooled solely for the game. The pony was ridden around for a while and as its rider dismounted it was obvious that he was '. . . absolutely flabbergasted!' The reason? 'Because', he said, 'that horse can do more in the way of dressage than any of my horses that are specifically schooled to it!'

During the sixties the Queen was breeding would-be polo ponies for the Prince at Windsor out of some of his retired pony mares, but for various reasons they were seldom a success with him and few ended up in the role for which they were destined. Some were sold, one to the Maharajah of Jaipur. One that grew too big for the game was Doublet, who became world famous by carrying Princess Anne to victory in the 1971 European eventing championships at Burghley.

Most Argentine polo ponies are sired by English Thoroughbreds but are out of native mares and tend to be stockier, slightly heavier and usually calmer than blood ponies. And while nothing can be better than a Thoroughbred pony with the right disposition, the Prince found that if the Argentine ponies were wanting in speed they made up for it in handiness, and in temperament were often more co-operative and suited to the game. Even the famous Betaway, the blood pony bred by the late Lord Rosebery that was the star of Prince Philip's string during the sixties, had to be ridden and treated with the utmost tact.

Nowadays, Prince Charles plays ponies that are almost all home-bred, and has the same advantage his father enjoyed of having

Prince Philip displaying fine control of his pony in a game at Windsor in July 1968.

them schooled by an expert in what is a very difficult art. Prince Philip's ponies were schooled for years by the late Lord Mountbatten's rough rider who was a brilliant trainer. And even in the last two years when his trainer felt he was too old to be involved with the arduous job of training ponies from scratch, he still ordered the requisite exercise and work for those that were already made.

The Queen moves among members of the public stamping down divots kicked up by the ponies during the Royal Windsor Polo Tournament in June 1955.

During the years of his polo-playing Prince Philip did little other riding. As his public commitments rapidly expanded, his leisure time inevitably dwindled. What he had was fully taken up with playing matches or practising on the lawn at Windsor, where the Queen frequently trod in the divots afterwards. In the earlier days the Prince occasionally had fun utilising one of the riding horses for knocking a ball about, in particular Pegasus, an Anglo-Arab both the Queen and he rode, and one recalled as: 'A very vain horse – always very pleased with himself!' After giving up polo he kept a couple of ponies for a short while, to ride when keeping in touch with the game he loved by acting occasionally as umpire – until, as he remarks with a grin, 'the players got so rude I decided to give it up!'

With polo 'out' the Prince began looking for another suitable sport to take its place, and the one that has become an absorbing new hobby came about through his presidency of the FEI (the Fédération Equestre Internationale, anglicised to the International Equestrian Federation).

The FEI was formed in 1921 to act as the official governing body of equestrian sports, with a headquarters then in Brussels but now in Berne. The federation has a judges' panel, sending a foreign judge and technical delegate to each international show and, being completely authoritative, is strict in the enforcement of its rules.

Prince Philip was voted to succeed Prince Bernhard of the Netherlands as president in 1964. He accepted principally because, although polo was his métier he knew enough about horses and riding in general to understand what was being discussed, and could be a neutral chairman between the dressage, show-jumping and three-day eventing factions in the federation.

In the years since then there has been an explosion in horse activities everywhere, including the world of international competing. One of the problems for the FEI, therefore, has been trying to cope with the increasing number of countries taking part – from 30 when the Prince became president to around 70 today. To illustrate the size of the problem he quotes the annual fixture list, then a mere couple of pages of foolscap that has now swelled to a thick volume. On top of that is the large increase in the number of relative subjects for which the FEI is now responsible. In 1964 there were no veterinary regulations for international competitions and no rules for juniors or their ponies. 'Young Riders' was not then a recognised category and in Britain driving, competitive or otherwise, was either non-existent or so much in its infancy that the question of inclusion did not arise. All these facets of international competing now have their own rules introduced and enforced by the federation. Long-distance riding is being introduced with international vaulting waiting on the side-lines.

The uninitiated may not always be aware that one area in which the FEI has complete control, is in determining maximum height and spread of fences, and the number of drop and combined fences, allowed in both international three-day events and where applicable in show-jumping competitions, including those for juniors in both spheres. Prince Philip understandably gets a little irritated with journalists and others who query the 'increasingly formidable' courses without having first studied the relevant FEI rule book. They would then discover that these limits have remained unchanged for many years except that the maximum height for Olympic fences has now been lowered. What has changed is the number of times horses are expected to compete and the fact that competitors try harder. As the Prince so rightly points out, in the case of a three-day event the horse has got to be ridden over the cross-country course in a way that takes into account the conditions prevailing on the day.

A few years ago the course at Lexington, in the States, was under fire, with ugly stories of exhausted and disabled horses. Yet the Canadians, who won the team event, all got round without undue trouble. Their first rider, a girl going off in the unenviable position of trail-blazer, took the course fairly easily and went clear. On her return she warned her team-mates to 'watch it!' The conditions were hot and wet, and they would have to ride with sense and sensitivity and not rush round. The other Canadian team members took her advice and all got round, but there were some riders who stupidly disregarded the prevailing conditions and their unfortunate horses suffered accordingly. That is a case in point in which the course-builders were not to blame, but the riders and their chefs d'équipes, who should have been alert to the climatic conditions and recognised the problems, most certainly were.

Prince Philip, in his capacity as president of the FEI, was

The Queen presenting a tankard to the Duke of Edinburgh – a member of the winning Friar Park team in an invitation polo match against Silver Leys on Smith's Lawn in Windsor Great Park in June 1957.

involved in the apprehension being expressed from some quarters about the conditions to be encountered for the three-day event in Los Angeles, the venue for the next Olympics. While he was fully aware that it would be hot and sticky, the going in places undesirably rocky or sandy, there is nothing he or anybody else could do to change these factors, they are an integral part of the terrain and its climate. As always it would be up to the riders to adapt their tactics accordingly. If at any time they do not and there is further public disquiet about the effects on their horses, then the Prince considers they are likely to ruin their own sport by their own stupidity. But the question of smog was another matter – no amount of skilful course-riding could compensate for that and horses competing in the endurance events could not possibly be subjected to such a hazard. Prince Philip was thankfully able to announce that the International Equestrian Federation had decided that the cross-country events in the 1984 Olympic Games would be held 110 miles south of Los Angeles, on a ranch near the Pacific Ocean. The dressage and other equestrian events would still be held in the city.

      The eventing rules laid down by the FEI cover all phases of a three-day-event, including the time limits for the 'roads and tracks'. At one stage the question of doing away with this phase was raised, principally by the organisers who were getting bored with what is admittedly an unspectacular part of the competition, backed up by those whose interests lie in promoting the public interest. However, the

One of Prince Philip's last games at Smith's Lawn.

Prince Philip chatting with the Queen after umpiring a polo game at Windsor.

idea was quashed because this phase has always served a useful purpose.

When Prince Philip was still playing polo his ponies used to go the several miles from their stables to Smith's Lawn on their own four feet, so when they arrived they were warmed up and going well before starting what is very strenuous exercise. This would not have been the case if the ponies had been transported by box. For the same reason they did not return after the game by transport as that might well have meant their arriving back temporarily unsound, but were ridden quietly home, so ensuring that any stiffness due to minor bumps and bruises was removed by the exercise.

The same theory is applied to the roads-and-tracks phase of an event, where the effort required for the speed, endurance and cross-country phase of the second day has to be taken into account. The first 4,400 metres of 'roads and tracks' present few problems and the speed, never demanding, has now been reduced. The horses then arrive loosened up and ready for the steeplechase – at Badminton and Burghley a circuit of some 2760 metres long. In England this circuit gives some of the changes of direction always present on continental courses, and often includes some of the types of fences encountered abroad as well as the English uniform point-to-point jumps. By FEI regulations the fixed and solid part of the steeplechase obstacle 'shall not exceed one metre', and brush fences may not exceed an overall height of 1.4 metres – by no stretch of the imagination can that be considered an excessive height!

The second phase of 'roads and tracks' comes at the end of the steeplechase and these 9,900 metres present a different problem. By this time, the horse, however fit, will be blowing and sweating and has to be ridden accordingly, that is without incurring too many time penalties while at the same time nursing the animal for the exertions of the near 7000-metre course with around 30 fences that comes after a 10-minute rest and veterinary inspection.

Most years before Badminton and Burghley there are gloomy journalistic prophecies about some of the cross-country fences – at Badminton they usually include the eye-catching ski-jump and notorious quarry as well as any new and outstanding versions of the course-builder's art. But again no mention is made that under federation rules the fixed and solid part of all cross-country obstacles may not exceed a height of 1.2 metres, and only 50 per cent of those obstacles may be at maximum height.

Badminton, in the spring, and Burghley, in the autumn, are the two top-notch three-day events in Britain and competitors there come under the eagle eye of the selectors of national and international teams and individual riders, looking for form. This equestrian version of the pentathlon is intended to be a comprehensive test of all-round horsemanship and almost every activity of which the horse is capable, and it is geared to the top-flight combinations of horse and rider. Ideally the venue should be changed each year but this is obviously impossible, not least because of the thousands of spectators who now flock to these trials and can be accommodated in the wide and beautiful spaces of the Badminton and Burghley estates. The skill of the course-builder is therefore further stretched each year to build new fences, the majority with alternatives to challenge the initiative of riders who can interpret the relative difficulties of each, according to the capabilities of their horses on the day.

The FEI regulations also cover the standards for all the junior events, and the same applies to show-jumping. The maximum standards of height and width for different competitions remain constant, and it is up to the course-builders to vary fences within the limits of the regulations so that the courses are fair and jumpable – in national and international competitions by the top-class horse and rider – while making it possible for the best combination to win. Some people seem to think that the standards should be such that the average combination of horse and rider might have a chance of winning, but that misses the point. A course at world or Olympic standard has got to be one that the very best will win.

For years now a continuing argument with which Prince Philip and the federation have had to grapple concerns the use of drugs. This is not quite the same sort of 'doping' problem that at one time bedevilled the racing world, but is an infinitely complex subject that concerns a number of substances. Of these, Phenylbutazone ('Bute') is the one most familiar to the general public. Many horse-owners think of 'Bute' as a pain-killer, like a local anaesthetic, when it is in fact a therapy.

Like all polo ponies, Prince Philip's sometimes got a knock during a match, developing over the years slight aches and pains and arthritic conditions for which they were given 'Bute' because that is the therapy for those conditions. In recent years, having discovered the drug works on that kind of inflammation, people began to assume it would work on any kind of inflamed condition. It may do so, but such a condition can be due to a number of things, perhaps to an infection, and the true purpose of 'Bute' is curative in troubles arising from knocks, bangs, and twists. It is certainly not the panacea for most ills some people came to believe and should never be used as a preventative in case a horse should knock itself on, say, the cross-country phase of an event.

Looking back, the Prince is convinced a lot of horses did suffer badly from the overuse and misuse of Phenylbutazone, but he and the FEI felt that banning it altogether would be likely to give rise to something even less desirable such as de-nerving. There is another problem, common to those drugs that used wrongly are unacceptable, but are otherwise an acknowledged method of treating certain conditions. If such a drug were used perfectly correctly a few days before a competition, some horses would still show traces of it in a blood sample on the day, and because these are forbidden substances the animal would be disqualified. As Prince Philip says, that would obviously be nonsensical and so a reasonable compromise has to be evolved.

Since 1980, therefore, the FEI has tolerated a fixed maximum permissible level of Phenylbutazone in the blood of a horse for international competitions. There was considerable controversy amongst the British, German, and American vets as to what the 'permissible level' should be, but an agreement was reached and seems to be working. In the future it is hoped it may be possible to extend it to cover a number of other middle-of-the-road medications.

Not all the work of the FEI is concerned with such controversial problems as these, but the responsibilities are now so widespread that the office of president, for one who never accepts such a title unless he can become actively involved, is no sinecure. The work and travelling involved reduces still further the commodity of which Prince Philip is most short – time. But he finds it all intensely interesting and rewarding and in 1970 the FEI was instrumental in giving him the idea of the pastime that took over from polo.

Chapter Six

Carriage Driving

PRINCE PHILIP's involvement with competitive carriage-driving came about through a casual conversation at one of the FEI assemblies when Eric Brabec, a Polish delegate, suggested that the federation might draw up some rules for international driving. Initially sceptical but, in view of the number of his own 'brilliant ideas' rejected over the years, willing to consider anything bar the ridiculous, the Prince started to investigate the idea.

In Britain, driving horses and ponies was becoming increasingly popular but there were then no competitions as such. The few coaching classes and those for harness horses, organised by the British Driving Society at one or two shows that Prince Philip had seen, did not appear to offer much basis for what was in mind. However, he soon discovered that on the Continent there were a number of thriving four-in-hand trials comprising dressage and cross-country. In some, drivers from different countries competed against each other. Each competition had its own set of rules. He was already interested when a visit to the Aachen Horse Show where he saw 24 four-in-hands in the ring completed the conversion, and Prince Philip got moving with characteristic enthusiasm.

He persuaded Sir Mike Ansell, a personal friend and a member of the FEI executive committee, who had been prominent in the horse world for many years, to see if anything could be done. Sir Mike wasted no time in mustering all the top European driving enthusiasts at Berne, where he picked their brains and worked them off their feet, and was able to return with an agreed outline for the required type of competition. It was loosely based on the ridden three-day event. Then, in 1970, shortly after the first English driving competition for four-in-hands had taken place at Windsor, with a few pages of untried rules and without experience or such necessities as qualified organisers, judges, or time-keepers, the Swiss Federation put on the first ever international driving competition, in Lucerne. Representing Great Britain at the invitation of the FEI was Sir John Miller, the Crown Equerry, a keen whip who had been driving four-in-hands from the Royal Mews since the early sixties and had come second at Windsor. He gave an enthusiastic report to Prince Philip and from then on competition carriage-driving was 'in'.

Originally, the rules were designed for teams of four horses or ponies but they have now been adapted for pairs, tandems, and single

Prince Philip competes in the Marathon at the 1981 National Carriage Driving Championships in Windsor Great Park.

harness. Many of the refinements to the rules concerning the three different competitions, listed below, that comprise a full-scale driving contest, are based on Sir John's early experiences.

The competitions, a combination of any of them called a Combined Driving Competition, are as follows:

Competition A

Section 1 Presentation – with marks awarded for turnout, including harness, spares to be carried etc., and condition and matching of horses.
Section 2 Dressage – requiring the execution of specified movements at walk, working, collected and extended trot; a halt at a designed spot; and a rein-back.

Competition B

Marathon – comprising a cross-country course divided into five sections, each to be completed in a prescribed time, two at the walk, the others at different speeds of trot. There are a number of hazards to be negotiated, and a carriage and four must carry at least four people, one of them a referee.

Competition C

Obstacle driving – comprising accuracy in negotiating 18 pairs of cones set at 30 cm wider than the track width of the carriage, within a fairly tight time limit. (This section equates to the show-jumping phase of a ridden event.)

The FEI rules apply only to international competitions, and national federations arrange competitions under their own rules to fit their own circumstances.

It was in 1970 that Prince Philip was 50, the age at which he had decided to give up polo. He was still on the lookout for something to take its place and it seemed that this sport which he had been instrumental in setting up might be just what was required. The idea was strengthened in 1971 when he attended the Windsor Horse Show, where it had been agreed to put on an international driving competition for four-in-hands. In the autumn of that year the Prince went to Budapest to watch the first European driving championships, organised by the Hungarians.

In 1972, having gone round the marathon course of the international driving championships held at Windsor when acting as referee for Sandor Fülop, a Hungarian competitor, the Prince made up his mind: driving should be his new pastime and top-level competition a goal to be achieved as quickly as possible.

One of the deciding factors was that of economy. All the accessories – horses, carriages, coachmen, and grooms – were already to hand in the Royal Mews. So long as he utilised the horses normally

Prince Philip competing with the Queen's team of bays in the dressage section of the International Driving Grand Prix at the Royal Windsor Horse Show at Home Park in May 1981.

September 1981 at Windsor Great Park. Prince Philip and the timekeeper, Mrs Pauline Booth-Jones, negotiate the pond in Section A of the Marathon at the National Carriage Driving Championships.

available for state occasions, when not required for those duties, there would be little extra expense either for himself or for the mews.

Until this new interest began to take hold, Prince Philip's driving had been confined to the occasional outing at Balmoral when he used pony power for transport. In 1972 when he started taking a serious interest, he chose characteristically to embark on learning his new sport with a pair instead of the easier single-harness horse. In May of that year the Prince drove a carriage and pair at the Royal Windsor Horse Show. He then practised driving a pair of ponies at Balmoral and soon, a book of instructions in hand and with a mixed team of Highlands, Fells, and Haflingers, he set out to experiment with driving a four-in-hand.

In January 1973 Prince Philip took six bays from the Royal Mews to Sandringham and started training them and himself during the following weeks. He considers he was very lucky then in having the invaluable help of Major Tommy Thompson, recently retired as riding master of the Household Cavalry, who had ridden in three-day events, including Badminton, from 1949 to 1953, and was an experienced coaching whip. (Major Thompson joined the Royal Mews in 1971 and retired in 1979.) The Prince has of course always been able to draw on the excellent assistance and wide experience of the Crown Equerry.

For that 1973 season Prince Philip's team was drawn from two part-bred Cleveland Bays – Buttercup, a mare, and Fort Steel, a gelding – the pure-bred Cleveland Bay gelding, Doric, and Castlegar and Cadagon, two geldings that were bred by the late Sir Dymoke White.

Prince Philip tried his team out by competing at Lowther in April of that year and a month later fate decreed that the second ever European International Driving Championships should be held at

LEFT: *Prince Philip in immaculate turnout for the dressage section of a competition.*

RIGHT: *Prince Philip manoeuvring his four-in-hand through the sandpit obstacle during a Marathon.*

Windsor. This meant that the second driving competition of the Prince's life would be a top-level one. It was encouraging to come sixth in the presentation and dressage phase, and he was one of the only three to go clear in the obstacle driving, taking second place in that section. Sadly, he had hit the last of the hazards on the cross-country and had to retire with a bent carriage, giving him 17th place overall out of 19. The Prince did not feel it was a very good start.

Since that ambitious beginning he has had consistent success in the dressage and obstacle driving phases. Through the years he has been an individual competitor in the championships, and a member of the British team in 1979, 1980, and 1981 when he came 10th, one point behind a team-mate, in the European Championships. In 1981 there were also wins overall at Norwich and Tatton Park, but although he had come second on four occasions at Windsor, it was 1982 before he managed to win the International Driving Grand Prix on his home ground. This win, combined with his good and consistent competing record, brought

Prince Philip showing his skill in a smooth turn.

him a well deserved place in Britain's team for the 1982 World Driving Championships at Apeldoorn, in Holland, where he finished sixth after some trouble on the cross-country.

Like Princess Anne, Prince Philip's public commitments preclude him from putting in anything approaching the practice time the majority of his fellow competitors consider essential, and it is even more to his credit that he is now counted amongst the band of top international drivers. His dressage scores are consistently recorded at the top of the international scale and he is deadly accurate in the obstacle (cone) driving, although like all competitors he does occasionally have his share of trouble at some marathon obstacles.

Occasionally, the Prince starts the year with six horses in training, but usually with only the four plus one reserve, that are allowed to be taken to competitions. During January he moves them to Sandringham, to drive perhaps three or four days a week. There, one of the problems encountered when out driving on Sunday afternoons can be the amateur photographers who stand in the road to get a better view, but this is something to which driver and horses are now accustomed and much good schooling is accomplished on and around the estate. At Windsor, where the Prince manages to fit in training sessions during the Easter holiday and at some weekends, a few of the young horses with older ones are sometimes driven to stand around and listen at the various barracks during the ceremony of the Changing of the Guard. This is a practice that is also good training for the team's state occasions.

In one way the horses that Prince Philip and the Crown Equerry drive are unique. No other teams have to co-operate to the extent they do, distinguishing between drawing a historic carriage at a sedate trot down the Mall and cracking along rough tracks through a German wood with a complicated 'hazard' to negotiate en route. But whether ceremonial duty helps with the competitive work or vice versa, it is hard to say. Prince Philip thinks the ceremonial work must get his horses more acclimatised to crowds, although oddly enough, when competing, his

A sunny day for Prince Philip in the International Driving Grand Prix in May 1982.

team does not appear to be much better behaved in public than any of the others. In a sense the horses' state duties do present a slight difficulty, because then they are mixed in and put together in unfamiliar teams, and driven by strange drivers whose technique may be different. Obviously the conditions are very different, the carriages heavier, the whole system dissimilar from the competitive one, and it is probably right to say that in some ways the ceremonial work gives the horses an advantage and in some ways it does not.

On the other hand, the horses trained for competitive work are very much fitter than those used exclusively in London, something that could also cut both ways. If they are reasonably calm and sensible in training for driving events that should be of help in their public duties. If a horse is likely to 'take off' it is more likely to do so during the cross-country phase of a competition than at the sight of Green Park. The dressage training they receive is undoubtedly beneficial to their cere-monial work. When studying some of the photographs taken of the royal wedding processions, Sir John was pleased to note how they illustrated the good effects of the training the carriage horses receive for both competitive and ceremonial work. The four horses that took Prince Charles to St Paul's and brought him and his bride back to the palace after the service, were a team of Windsor Greys with which the Crown Equerry had often competed. They were postillion ridden, a method of control that clearly shows up an off-leader that pulls. The postillion rides the near-side horse, and if he has to hold back his led horse the animal turns its head in towards him. It was very satisfactory to have photo-graphic proof that all four horses were holding their heads perfectly level.

Originally, Prince Philip decided he would try to compete once a month during the season, that is for the four months of April, May, June, and July. Those would all be ordinary competitions, all sited in Britain, but since then he has been driving in either the European or World Championships as well, adding an extra one per year. A National Championship has now been introduced in September, so that for various reasons the Prince went to nine competitions in 1981, but was not contemplating quite so many for 1982.

He thoroughly enjoys driving once a year on the Continent, finding it both fun and interesting to get to a number of unlikely places he would otherwise never see. Driving in Hungary, Switzerland, Holland, and Poland (now sadly likely to be left out for the time being), as well as in Britain, he meets a lot of people, and since carriage drivers seem to be a long-lived breed, they keep meeting up, both as friends and as rival competitors. It is a very entertaining business, always with plenty to talk about – different carriages, types of harness, and since, competitively speaking, drivers outlive their horses, different teams as well.

For this last reason the names at the top of the sport may suddenly change. The horses driven by a man who has been virtually unbeatable for years grow old and he often has to replace them with a younger team. Whereas an event rider has to get to know just one horse at a time, a driver has got to understand the psychology of his team and that means understanding five animals, including the reserve horse, that however close in looks and breeding will still have individual personalities – including as often as not, some irritating personal habits. The horses driven in pairs and teams have to move side by side harmoniously, operating together to do a fair share of the work. For some obscurely equine reason the leaders often delight in nagging (trying to bite) each other, a distracting habit seldom indulged by the wheelers, who frequently have a vice of their own – leaning or pulling away from each other.

Prince Philip finds he has to have even more rapport with the horses he drives than is necessary for a rider, who only has to cope with one animal, one temperament, one idiosyncrasy. If all five of you – your four horses and yourself – do not operate as a team 'the thing doesn't function'.

One sideline connected with his competing that the Prince finds of interest is the opportunity to study the abilities and characteristics of the many different breeds of horse that compete – a subject on which he enlarges in his own excellent book, *Competition Carriage Driving*, published in 1982. The team he drives today, three of them mares, are the home-bred progeny, by Cleveland Bay sires, out of some of the Oldenburg mares Sir John Miller drove in the early seventies. He finds these horses perhaps a little bigger than he would choose, but with very good paces and both fast and intelligent. He comes up against teams of Welsh Cobs, strong and courageous, capable of being capricious but with a skilled driver always giving a good account of themselves. There are the Hackneys, the only breed of English carriage horse, apart from the

Prince Philip with his team at the Windsor Horse Show.

Cleveland Bay. Bred for looks and speed, they are the ballerinas of the show ring and can also do well in driving trials with a driver who can handle them. The Prince comes across Friesians, the Dutch horses that are not unlike large-size Fell ponies, and the consistently placed animals of Trackehnen type. Some of his opponents drive Holsteins or Hanoverians, similar German breeds of classic carriage horses that perform well, especially in the dressage phase but owing to their large size sometimes have difficulty in negotiating certain marathon hazards. Imre Abonyi, the Hungarian who was European Driving Champion in 1971 and dominated the scene for years, drove native Hungarian horses, and after 1971 mostly pure-bred Lipizzaners. Georgi Bardos, Abonyi's compatriot who supplanted him to become reigning world champion, also drives a team of pure Lipizzaners, a breed that by tradition and ancestry should be ideal for the work. For although Lipizzaners come from six lines of stallions and eighteen families of mares, they share the same willing, equable temperament, and the strength and endurance that the Piber-bred stallions demonstrate with performances of haute école at the famous Spanish Riding School in Vienna.

Nowadays, in addition to seeing different breeds of horse competing, Prince Philip has opportunities for studying breeds of ponies. Even on the Continent, in countries not formally considered to be 'pony minded', driving four-in-hands of ponies is catching on, and in 1980 there was a class in the driving trials at the Royal Windsor Show for pony teams, instead of for the horse pairs of previous years.

For all his prowess with his horses the Prince does not neglect the royal ponies. When in Scotland he has been driving a team of them for fun for about eight years. In 1982 he put a team of Fells together and found they went extremely well, taking third place in the trials at Scone. Later in the same year he won with them at Floors Castle, Kelso, and at Lowther. He also finds the keen rivalry and competitiveness of the pony events and their outcome very interesting, and it is obviously more convenient and economical when at Balmoral to drive the ponies to local events rather than bring the horses all the way up from Windsor.

In the previous year Prince Philip drove a pair of Fells to a very close second place in private trials, by invitation only, for singles and pairs, organised at Balmoral 'to encourage the already evident enthusiasm for driving in the North East of Scotland.' That was when the lucky competitors, on the evening of the second day, were invited 'to see the Prince and Princess of Wales home from their honeymoon.' They were able to watch a procession to the castle when the Prince and the Princess's heather-covered landau was pulled by estate workers, to the accompaniment of pipes and the spirited notes of a hunting horn expertly rendered by Sir John Miller.

Through driving both horses and ponies Prince Philip has discovered that the two species are very different and, contrary to what some might suppose, driving ponies is more difficult than driving horses. In a sport where any adversities usually happen very quickly, ponies produce reactions at a speed to match, frequently doing something totally unexpected and quite often entirely illogical. Like ponies, horses vary a great deal according to their breed and individual characteristics, but tend to be calmer by temperament and slower reacting, giving the driver a little more time to attempt the necessary counteractions.

The Prince finds his Fells tough and willing, and very speedy which is surprising for their appearance has been described as 'unwieldly'. In character they can be a bit dour but the good ones possess a quality that in this sport is invaluable – come what may, they are unflappable. The Haflingers are even tougher and need urging to develop their speed. As a breed they can be too clever, becoming easily bored, but although like most ponies they are distinctly independent minded, Haflingers enjoy and respond to a challenge.

The regulations for a carriage used with a four-in-hand for competitive driving demand that it should be of a fixed minimum weight and must possess four wheels. Otherwise there are no regulations concerning the vehicle used in the marathon, and a great variety of modern, experimental, and conventional carriages are used. Years ago, when Prince Philip was driving at Lowther he was using a splendid old wooden vehicle known as the Balmoral dogcart. Such a vehicle would be useless for the present-day conditions of the marathon, and he now has a metal-framed carriage with a metal pole that stands up well to such exigencies.

People sometimes allude to Prince Philip's sport as 'this dangerous driving thing' – a description he considers unjustified. As with most strenuous sports and hobbies, particularly those in which horses are involved, there are occasional accidents and injuries but considering the number of drivers today and the number of driving events, they are relatively few. As he so rightly says in his book, how can one define what is dangerous? There are people who cannot be trusted with a bicycle! He finds his sport exciting and rewarding but one that, provided it is undertaken sensibly and with the proper precautions, cannot be called dangerous.

One safeguard that should be observed is to get rid of any leader in the team that pulls, unless the habit can be remedied by different bitting or some others means. Hazards are sufficiently difficult without a pulling horse, although on the occasion when the Prince's referee baled out from the seat beside him, no hazard was in fact involved. As Prince Philip later assured him, it was a case of most prudent departure, on a steep hill with wet, slippery grass where Philip was grappling, not entirely successfully, with a leader that insisted on pulling, even downhill.

Turning over a carriage is not as frequent an occurrence as it used to be before the vehicles were built with a lower centre of gravity, but the Prince has twice experienced what he describes as 'this undignified process'. On one occasion it was in Hungary and again a pulling leader was involved. The horse took such quick and violent exception to the sudden appearance of a pair of huge, long-horned Hungarian cattle that it pulled the whole team up against the side of the hazard they were negotiating. Inevitably the wheels rode up the side of this solidly constructed affair and over they went, Prince Philip on top of the referee who unintentionally cushioned his fall. As a good driver, despite being flat on his back the Prince hung on to the reins, the grooms were down and away to the horses' heads like a flash and the team stopped – which, with the vast expanses of the Hungarian plains to hand, was just as well.

Although from the spectator point of view the water hazards are spectacular, Prince Philip has not had any great problems with those encountered during competitions, but during training water has sometimes occasioned food for thought. In the beginning, his horses made it plain that getting their feet wet on rain-soaked London streets was one thing, but being expected to keep going through crossings where the water might well be knee-deep was another. One of the first lessons was to get them, a pair at a time, to cross a small stream. One pair had already been ridden through it, but then in true equine fashion declined to take the same route pulling a conveyance. When the time-honoured method failed, of sitting it out in the hope that the horses would get bored first, the Prince dispatched Major Thompson to the further bank with a jar of sugar-lumps providentially discovered under the seat. This was a device often used to provide a reward, or to promote good relations when visiting the stables, and the rattling of sugar was a familiar and appreciated sound.

At the first shake one horse pricked up its ears and took notice, then suddenly decided it was worth the plunge. The more timid animal went forward too from habit, then realised what was happening and tried to stop. The other horse went on and the carriage swung downstream heading for a bridge too low to accommodate a swan. At the same moment that Prince Philip realised there was no room for the carriage to turn, it seemed to occur to the horses that the banks were too steep to climb and the greedier animal swung back and, taking its partner with it, walked to the enticing sugar jar – at least that is what the Prince assumed. He has a distinct impression of the alarm on the face of the unsuspecting guest who was his passenger that morning, but no recollection of taking any corrective action. Philip was sitting, eyes closed, awaiting the inevitable crack of the carriage pole breaking – an event which for some unknown reason did not occur.

When training at Sandringham at a later date, as there was no other suitable water-crossing a rudimentary ford had been bull-dozed across a drainage ditch in a water meadow, an operation the Prince had cause to admit later was not very sensible. By this time the horses were prepared to go through water, but the bottom of this ditch was deceptively soft. The leaders managed to flounder through but as the wheelers got to the water the front wheels of the carriage sank into the mud and they gave an almighty heave which broke their traces, leaving the reins as the only connection between themselves and their driver. Prince Philip found himself on the far side of the ditch, contemplating Major Thompson still seated in the abandoned carriage with a look of total disbelief on his face. Four large horses were careering round the water meadow shedding bits of harness as they went, and as one made for the gate and home it was met and secured by Princess Anne, as astonished by this apparition as the young event horse she was riding.

About the only time the Prince feared water might play a part in the performance of his team when competing was at the 1975 European Championships at the Baltic resort of Sopot, in Poland. The course included a section along the beach and through a foot of water under the pier, and it seemed only sensible to get the horses used to such unknown conditions. They were taken in pairs, and the first two were in trouble directly they got into the soft sand behind the beach. It was embarrassing trying to manhandle a pair of reluctant horses and a vehicle under the curious gaze of scantily clad sunbathers, and Prince Philip proceeded with more caution, and more success with his other two horses. After this they still had to perform as a team, and although the sand was accomplished safely, there was still the small matter of the sea. Nothing would induce the horses to paddle along the edge in a straight line, and their progress along the beach was marked out in a series of graceful hoof-marked loops as they followed the wavelets out, and then sidled in again with the next ones. True to what their driver aptly describes as 'the incomprehensible equine thought processes', on the actual day the team went through the water and under the pier as though this were their normal route when being driven for the opening of Parliament.

Since polo is a game and driving a totally different form of sport, it is impossible to compare the different skills and challenges required and as both pastimes were undertaken at a very different age, it would be illogical to try and assess which Prince Philip finds the most enjoyable. Certainly he has brought the same enthusiasm and involvement of his polo-playing days to the years he has been driving.

Like three-day eventing on which it was modelled, one of the great attractions of competitive driving is the variety provided by the different phases, but as Prince Philip says, the appeal of each phase varies from one event to another. On one day you can get a great deal of satisfaction from doing a good dressage test – and although he considers every civilised horse should be capable of the kind of compulsory movements that, basically, demand little more than accuracy and obedience, that does not always happen. There are days when it is cold and wet, the reins slip, you forget the test, and wish you had never started. You can have a filthy wet cross-country and it is misery all the way round. Or you have a lovely day up in the Lake District and it is such a pleasure driving about in the countryside that it is difficult to pay attention to what you are doing . . . because you are admiring the view. On one occasion everything goes right in the 'cones' phase; on another things could not go more wrong.

There are of course many times when all the phases are enjoyable, as proved by Prince Philip's own successes, and generally the standard at the top levels of this sport is very even, adding to the overall excitement. At the 1981 championships there were only about 20 points between the first twelve competitors.

The Prince has the satisfaction of knowing that his own participation and pleasure in competitive driving has helped popularise the sport he initiated. It has still not quite 'caught on' with the public, chiefly because the media do not yet quite understand it or fully appreciate the attractions for television. Much the same occurred in the early days of ridden eventing, now a sport that at the top levels is a tremendous 'crowd and audience puller'. From the competitors' point of view driving is a thriving and quickly expanding sport. There is a great deal of interest in Australia, even more in the USA, and enquiries are continually coming in and spreading outwards from many parts of the world. Nor is it, as some imagine, a pastime that can only be indulged by those with the income to afford driving and maintaining a four-in-hand of horses. There are competitive events for singles and pairs, of both horses and ponies, and four-in-hands of ponies are rapidly gaining in popularity. Many driving clubs run 'friendly' one-day trials where the standards and the rules are not intended to emulate the heights of those run under FEI regulations.

A pair of ponies which Prince Philip enjoyed driving for fun when he first had them have now got an almost historical standing. These were two of the three Caspian ponies, a stallion and two mares, he was given when he offered to have them in England for breeding, as a genetic safeguard for the breed in case anything should happen in Iran, their country of origin, to jeopardise these rare little horses. The offer was made when the Prince and Princess Anne were representing the Queen at the late Shah's coronation celebrations, staged at Persepolis in 1971, and was to prove fortuitous.

The offer was accepted by Mrs Firoux, an American married to a Persian, who had found, in the spring of 1965, a small pony pulling a cart through the narrow alleys of the bazaar at Amol, near the Caspian Sea. Despite its appalling condition it appeared to belong to a specific, if unknown breed, and eventually she managed to find a few similar ponies in the same area and one or two on the north face of the Elburz range. It took her two years to find sufficient animals to establish a small breeding herd. In the meantime, extensive osteological and blood studies were suggesting what is now accepted, that this large-eyed, slim-legged little equine with horse rather than pony characteristics, is in direct descent from the ancient small Persian horse, thought to be extinct for two thousand years.

When Prince Philip met Mrs Firouz she had already established another small stud of Caspians in Bermuda, and before the collapse of Iran there was time for the breed to be built up in a few other places outside the country.

The Prince's Caspian ponies are kept at the stud where they were sent originally to be looked after and bred, and they and their progeny (which do not belong to him), have helped save a species that at the time of their discovery only numbered about 50. Since the Iranian revolution the chances of this little horse being developed and specifically bred in its native land can be reckoned as nil. As a serious and dedicated conservationist, it must give Prince Philip great satisfaction to know he has personally played an active part in preserving a historic species, once thought to be extinct.

Despite his general interest in horses and ponies and the fact that he was for a time president of the Hackney Society, the Prince has no direct connection with any of the British horse-breeding societies. He is, however, very interested in the efforts of Colonel Sir Harry Llewellyn – who during the fifties with his famous show-jumper, Foxhunter, represented Great Britain 35 times – to develop a British riding horse on the same lines adopted for many years by the Germans and French.

Few if any of the sort of animal that used to be known in England as a hunter now exist. This was the type once bred in the backyards of the many people who hunted and liked to produce their own horse, and would have been excellent for use in the show-jumping, dressage, and ridden and driven eventing worlds of today where foreign breeds now dominate.

The British breed societies have always registered and looked after their own breeds, but this has not always been the case with half-breds. For several years now the Cleveland Bay Society has been registering half-bred Clevelands of either sex, and more recently the Hunters Improvement Society has started a register of approved mares which there is hope of expanding – both steps in the right direction. Without something like the continental systems of registration and breeding Prince Philip feels Britain will continue to lose out on suitable competition horses, because it can still be very difficult to find a British cross-bred horse with an existing record of its breeding and collaterals.

The Prince has learned from his experience with his harness horses how important it is to know these things in order to assess what the animal's temperament may be. At one time different horses were bought for the mews from different countries and he himself was given a horse in Germany and another in Denmark. They looked similar but acquired like that there was no way of appraising their individual temperaments or knowing whether they would be compatible, a crucial factor, until they were put together as a pair. He has found it quite different now that he drives home-bred mares all with recognisably similar temperaments. He knows what he is handling and is not having to deal with four totally different characters, and he feels that an efficient selective system, whereby people could actually go and see what they are getting, is essential.

In 1957, acting on a suggestion by Sir Mike Ansell, Prince Philip agreed to lend his name to a Pony Club project he felt would provide fun and be of benefit to 'ordinary' club members riding 'ordinary' family ponies. This resulted in the Prince Philip Mounted Games, an enjoyable competition for which generations of Pony 'Clubbers' have had cause to be grateful. It had occurred to him that as the standards of Pony Club competition rose with the years, those average young riders unable to afford high-class ponies were going to be left out, a surmise that could have proved to be very true. Nowadays, the levels at which the top-notch Pony Club members compete in the inter-branch show-jumping, eventing, and other mounted sports is so high, the riders' ability and the quality of their mounts, which are principally horses, so marked, that the mounted games, with their age limit for the riders and height limit for the ponies, becomes yearly more welcome.

In the past ten years the quality of skills and speed developed in the games has also greatly risen but, thanks to those who train the teams, without losing the fun and original team spirit. And while from time to time over-enthusiasm has resulted in distasteful rough riding, this has not gone unmarked by Pony Club officials. In all the branches many junior members still thoroughly enjoy doing their best to qualify for a team to contest the area games. And nowadays the co-operation and dash of the speedy little ponies taking part in the grand finale for the run-off of the Prince Philip Cup, at the Horse of the Year Show, is matched by the ability and keenness of their riders, spurred on by the vociferous enthusiasm of the spectators.

The thought that resulted in the mounted games that bear his name stems from the interest in the 'animal on four legs' Prince Philip shares with the Queen, even though their interests take different forms. Those of the Prince lie principally with his driving and the work and problems of the FEI with all its off-shoots. The Queen's involvement

The Duke of Edinburgh taking Mrs Nancy Reagan on a carriage drive through Windsor Home Park in June 1982.

with horses lies mainly with breeding the various types and with her own specialised racing interests. She always enjoys watching Prince Philip when he is competing at Windsor, just as she used to enjoy watching him play polo, but although he accompanies the Queen to the Derby and to Ascot, racing is not really his forte. Like their children, Prince Philip prefers participating to being a spectator, and Queen Elizabeth the Queen Mother is the one member of the family who shares whole-heartedly, if again from a slightly different angle, in the Queen's feeling for the 'sport of kings'.

BELOW AND RIGHT: *A decade before the Russian invasion of Afghanistan Prince Philip's horse interests and excellent photography enabled him to capture for posterity pictures of top-notch Afghan horsemen playing buzkashi. This was the rough, tough equestrian sport where whips could be used on opponents, but never on their horses, and the 'ball' was usually a headless goat.*

Pictures from the Duke of Edinburgh's own collection.

Chapter Seven

Royal Racing

THERE IS a delightful photograph of Queen Elizabeth the Queen Mother when she was a little girl, riding side-saddle on her pony in the grounds of her beautiful home, St Paul's Waldon Bury, in Hertfordshire. She has always been devoted to horses. A pony or donkey was invariably included amongst the numerous pets that were part of her happy childhood, but although she rode as a child there is no record of her continuing as she grew up. She did not hunt and in those days equestrian competition was virtually unknown outside the army.

When Queen Elizabeth, then the Lady Elizabeth Bowes-Lyon, married King George V's second son and became the Duchess of York, her interest in horses was fostered. The Duke kept a stable of hunters until he sold them in the interests of economy and their daughters were pony-lovers from the earliest age. As soon as Elizabeth, and then the younger Margaret, were old enough, their mother ensured they received correct instruction in the sport they so enjoyed. After the accession Queen Elizabeth loved to watch the King riding with his daughters in the Home Park at Windsor. Occasionally, Elizabeth and Margaret had the treat of accompanying the Queen to a horse show, or on the annual outing to the Royal Tournament, where in those days horses figured even more prominently than they do today.

During World War II Queen Elizabeth shared the King's interest in his good flat-racing fillies and, like the princesses, always enjoyed going with him to visit his trainers. In 1946, when the Royal Stud was beginning to pick up again after the lean war years, she shared the King's delight when his home-bred filly, Hypericum, despite bolting before the start, won the One Thousand Guineas.

Edward VII, both when Prince of Wales and when he was King, patronised steeplechasing, only organised as a sport at the beginning of the nineteenth century, but after he founded his Sandringham stud his main interest lay in flat-racing which the British royal family have supported for so many hundreds of years. It was only natural that King George VI should continue to concentrate on flat-racing, and during those post-war years Queen Elizabeth's interest in the sport became considerably more than academic. It was a chance conversation that brought her into steeplechasing, a world of which she then knew very little.

King George VI and Queen Elizabeth attending the Oaks at Epsom on May 25 1950.

When the King's filly, Avila, won the Coronation Stakes at Ascot in 1949 there had been more than the usual royal jubilation, because the filly's owner had recovered sufficiently from a recent operation to attend the race and watch her victory. During dinner at Windsor Castle that evening Lord Mildmay, an old friend of the family and champion National Hunt amateur jockey for the previous four seasons, was discussing the race, and then suggested that it would be fun for the Queen to branch out on her own and have a horse in training for jumping.

The idea appealed to both the Queen and Princess Elizabeth, then aged 23 and it was decided that they would share a suitable horse. Lord Mildmay was delighted to act as Queen Elizabeth's racing manager and his long-standing friend, Peter Cazalet, who trained all the Mildmay horses, became the first royal jumping trainer. It was a particularly happy set-up because the Queen herself had known the Cazalet family from a girlhood friendship with her contemporary, Thelma, now Mrs Cazalet-Keir. In those days she had also stayed at Fairlawne, the Cazalet's lovely estate near Shipbourne, in Kent, where the training stables had since been established. In years to come those visits were repeated with much enjoyment when she went to see her horses.

Monaveen was the chosen horse, a well bred eight-year-old with the blood of the 1920 Derby winner, Spion Kop, in his veins, but

The Queen Mother at the Cheltenham Races in March 1982.

whose previous existence had been a little chequered. Bred by an Irish farmer, as a three-year-old Monaveen had been set to pulling a milk float to quieten him down before being put up for sale. After training efforts at Epsom, which were not all that successful, and three falls on three different courses, the horse changed hands again after the war, for £35. A long rest and then the use of a hood (wide open 'cups' to help concentration) that he subsequently always wore for racing, produced the hoped-for results. In the autumn of 1948 Monaveen won two good races in a row and was sufficiently impressive to be entered for the 1949 Grand National. Unfortunately he fell in a preliminary race and his jockey broke an arm. Another jockey was injured the day before the National and Tony Grantham, Cazalet's stable jockey, was at the last minute given the ride on this horse he had never ridden before. Grantham found Monaveen's jumping on the first circuit so brilliant that, despite being shot out of the saddle by a bad peck at the nineteenth, the open ditch, he had no hesitation in recommending the horse to his 'guv'nor'.

After that there was a win at Folkestone in May and another well run race a month later. The first time Monaveen ran for his royal owners was at Fontwell Park in October 1949. He was ridden by Grantham and appeared in Princess Elizabeth's newly registered colours, the scarlet jacket, purple hooped sleeves, and black cap. After her accession she took on the colours of the reigning sovereign, the purple, scarlet sleeves and black cap with golden tassel that have so often honoured the flat-racing scene. Fontwell Park is not one of the grand tracks and the race was only a three-horse affair, but Monaveen won with ease, firing Queen Elizabeth's growing enthusiasm for the jumping game and the friendly informality of National Hunt racing.

Owing to the King's poor health the Queen was taking on an increasing number of public duties and was seldom able to watch Monaveen's racing career in person. But as part owner, Princess Elizabeth went when she could and was at Liverpool with Princess Margaret for the exciting occasion when the royal horse was only just beaten in the Grand Sefton steeplechase by Freebooter, an Aintree specialist. Obviously the newly instituted three-mile handicap called the Queen Elizabeth Chase was a special date for Monaveen, and although the Queen was unable to attend, Princess Elizabeth flew back from Malta where Prince Philip was stationed. After the race she was able to go on to Sandringham, where she was spending the New Year, and tell the King and Queen the thrilling news that Monaveen, out in front from the start, had set such a pace this time that he had won comfortably, defeating his rival, Freebooter.

In all, this first of the royal 'chasers was to win four important races as well as minor ones. He even came fifth in the 1950 Grand National – that was a great day for Aintree. The King had been well enough to accompany Queen Elizabeth and the princesses, and the royal party was as excited with the horse's running as the crowds cheering him on when Monaveen was one of the 7 to finish out of 49 starters.

With 75 winners Cazalet was the leading National Hunt trainer that season, for the first time, with Monaveen the stable's biggest winner in prize money, but tragedy was only round the corner. Lord Mildmay, at intervals liable to suffer agonising cramp in his neck, the legacy of an old racing injury, was drowned on an early morning swim when staying at his home at Mothecombe, in Devon. In that accident Peter Cazalet lost his greatest friend and owner and Queen Elizabeth her friend and racing manager. Perhaps the place Anthony Mildmay had won in the hearts of the racing world is best epitomised by an extract from a *Times* leading article, published the day after his memorial service: 'There never was a harder rider, a better loser or a more popular winner; and although he always valued the race more than the victory and the victory more than the prize, he would not perhaps have disdained the reward he has won – which is a kind of immortality amongst the English.'

Lord Abergavenny succeeded as Queen Elizabeth's racing manager and Manicou, bought from Cazalet who had been left all the Mildmay horses, joined the royal string. A five-year-old entire of exceptional temperament, the horse had won a brilliant race with Lord Mildmay only two months before his rider's death.

Princess Elizabeth, who was expecting her second child, had decided not to take a share in the horse. Manicou therefore appeared for the first time under royal ownership at the Fontwell November meeting, in Queen Elizabeth's own colours – the blue, buff stripes, blue sleeves, black cap and gold tassel – that had been those of her great-uncle, Lord Strathmore, a notable amateur rider of his day. Although Manicou's name was to be remembered almost more for his value at stud, in his only racing season – 1950–51 – he won three good races, including his last, the King George VI Chase, against older and proven horses. His first race over fences was at Kempton Park, in the Wimbledon Handicap Chase. Queen Elizabeth was there with Princess Elizabeth and Manicou's decisive win cheered the grey dampness of a November day – and maybe helped assuage to some degree the sadness of what happened only a week later.

Monaveen had been entered again in the Queen Elizabeth Chase to see if he could repeat his victory of the previous season. That time Queen Elizabeth was determined to go and watch if she possibly could, and she was there at Hurst Park when the first 'chaser of her racing life fell at the water jump, fortunately out of sight of the grandstand, and broke a leg so badly that he had to be put down straightaway.

This is one of the tragic hazards of steeplechasing that owners always pray they will not have to face. In the 34 years or so since Queen Elizabeth first entered the jumping game she has more than once had to cope with the same kind of situation as the loss of Monaveen. Each time she has done so in the same admirable way, tempering her own sadness with thought and sympathy for the others concerned – the jockey and trainer and the lad who has looked after the horse.

As the years slipped by towards the sixties there were other good horses to follow Monaveen and Manicou, and certainly Devon Loch, the fourth royal horse to come to Fairlawne, was one of them. He was also the horse whose mysterious and unbelievable fate was to bring his owner the greatest disappointment of her racing life. As a newcomer to running over fences, Devon Loch acquitted himself well in January 1952 but soon had to be rested, after damaging a tendon, until the 1954–55 season when he reappeared to win two top novice chases.

In Queen Elizabeth's yearly record of winners under National Hunt rules the seasons 1951–52 and 1952–53 are blank. King George VI died in his sleep in the early hours of February 6 1952 and for his wife much of life stopped too for a time.

Devon Loch, ridden by Dick Francis, now famous for his novels of the racing scene, lined up for the 1956 Grand National. For most of

The Queen Mother with Devon Loch after the 1956 Grand National.

those riding in it the Grand National is more of a worry than a delight, but for Dick Francis, until he was 50 yards from the post, the horse he was riding provided him with the sort of run jockeys dream about. Gradually passing horse after horse, Devon Loch's jumping became better and better and as they approached the Canal Turn they were lying a comfortable second. The horse jumped the last of those 30 fences as easily as if it had been the first. On the last few hundred yards he was well in front, still fresh after more than four miles and galloping fast, with only a few more strides to make him the most popular winner ever, in what would have been a record time. ESB, who won, broke the existing record. What happened next is racing history, the reasons never resolved. There was the strange leap with ears still pricked, the collapse onto his belly straddled in a position never seen in a horse before or since, the staggering up with hind legs that momentarily would not work, and, most strange of all, no perceptible after-effects. It could have been a muscle spasm or cramp, an inborn weakness, or the funnelling of the unparalleled roar of cheering into the horse's sensitive ears, as Dick Francis believes. No one knows, but when it happened it stilled Queen Elizabeth, the Queen, and the rest of the enraptured royal party, as well as those thousands of cheering spectators, certain of a royal victory, into horror-struck, incredulous silence. What is not generally known is that Devon Loch went on to race

A near miss at the Ascot races for the Queen Mother's horse.

again, both hurdling and over fences, with success, until retired to end his days as the trainer, Noel Murless's hack.

Queen Elizabeth has always had the greatest affection for all her horses but inevitably there have been the favourites. One at the top of the list was The Rip, bred by the landlord of The Red Cat at Wootton Marshes in Norfolk. He was out of an unrideable mare that was bought for 50 guineas and then sent to the local jumping stallion, the Queen Mother's retired 'chaser, Manicou. The resultant colt foal was a winner at every show he attended with his dam in the summer of 1955 and, on hearing this, the Queen Mother made an appointment to see Manicou's first son. It took place on the lawn of the pub and, pleased with the colt's appearance, she asked for first refusal. As the animal, then called Spoilt Union, grew to a yearling Queen Elizabeth often took a look at him when she was staying at Sandringham and eventually was able to buy him for 400 guineas.

Re-named The Rip, he went to Major Eldred Wilson, who broke in Queen Elizabeth's young horses, and he reported that the horse seemed 'rather a plain, clumsy, ponderous two-year-old'. All 'chasers have to be given time to mature and The Rip was a late developer. He began to improve when hunted as a four-year-old and went to Fairlawne in the late spring of 1959, making an inauspicious debut on the race-course six months later. He only won once when raced over hurdles, but grew into a fine 'chaser with the strength to clobber a fence and still survive. In his first eight seasons The Rip won 13 races for the Queen Mother and was placed 16 times.

Gay Record was a horse of special interest to his royal owner. He had not been difficult to break, but Major Wilson found him over-excitable in company when hunting. At Fairlawne he was so neurotic and difficult that he was sent back to Sandringham in disgrace, only returning for training as a six-year-old. Even then he intensely disliked going out in a string and was almost unmanageable, and if taken in a horsebox to the races worked himself up into a nervous lather. At the same time the horse appeared to have sufficient ability to make it worth while persevering with him, and Queen Elizabeth suggested he should go to the small Priory Stables at Reigate where the trainer, Jack O'Donoghue, special-ised in 'difficult' horses.

It was a suggestion that was to repay the originator in full. Gay Record eventually won eight races for Queen Elizabeth, including the Sevenoaks Chase at Folkestone in October 1964, when he was 12, that made him her 100th winner.

Although the Queen's breeding and racing interests lie with flat-racing and the Queen Mother's with steeplechasing, they share an enthusiasm for each other's sport that has been strengthened in some cases by the parentage of particular horses.

In the early days Queen Elizabeth's animals came mostly from Ireland, with some bought from France, including M'as-tu-vu and Laffy and then later, Worcran and the hurdler, Makaldar. There was a period

*The Queen Mother's horse
Laffy after a triumphant win at
the Ulster Harp National at
Downpatrick on April 6 1962.*

when stores, that is young horses, usually yearlings kept for some years
before racing, were bought cheaply in Ireland and spent some time at
Sandringham before going on to Major Wilson for breaking, and eventually to train at Fairlawne. It was disappointing that out of the 11 stores
bought over four years none were to show outstanding ability – with the
unexpected exception of Gay Record – and although Queen Elizabeth
loved seeing her young horses at Sandringham, the scheme was
abandoned. She began taking an interest in breeding her own jumping
stock in the late fifties. That was when she bought the five-year-old mare,
Queen of the Isle, at the same time as King of the Isle, a full brother. Like
most trainers, Cazalet did not like training mares as he felt they upset the
opposite sex, geldings and entires alike. When Queen of the Isle failed
her promise as a racehorse, she went to stud and became one of the
Queen Mother's outstanding brood mares, being the dam of Inch Arran,
Colonious, Isle of Man and Queen's College, between them winners of
over 40 races over jumps.

Charlot, who ran in the 1966–67 and 1967–68 seasons, was the
first home-bred winner of three good races. Reared at Sandringham he
was by the Queen's top-class horse, Doutelle, out of the Queen Mother's,
mare, Nicola, and so of mutual royal interest.

When Princess Anne began schooling Columbus it was a family
joke to say that she must keep the big grey out of sight of her grandmother
– or he would be whisked away and turned into a steeplechaser! And
certainly Colonist II, who fathered Columbus, sired a number of Queen
Elizabeth's good horses that were 'turned into 'chasers!' The Queen also
took great interest in Colonist's progeny as this rough, tough old customer

stood at Sandringham as one of the resident stallions for many years, and the Queen Mother had a double interest in the horse and his offspring. She and Sir Winston Churchill had had the two best novice hurdlers, her Makaldar and his Sun-Hat, in training at Fairlawne at the same time. Colonist II had been one of Sir Winston's best 'chasers, like his owner a real battler, and when Queen Elizabeth the Queen Mother heard the horse was being difficult to manage at Sir Winston's stud near Lingfield, she suggested that the Queen should buy him.

Of the horses Colonist sired for the Queen Mother, five had between them won 33 steeplechases and hurdle races by the end of the 1979–80 season, 14 of them by the good grey, Inch Arran, whose dam was Queen of the Isle, and the best Sandringham-bred horse, Cazalet trained. The last foal Colonist ever bred, at the age of 27, was Queen Elizabeth's Colonia, the dam of her Upton Grey, a winner of several races but now dead.

Colonello was one of the Colonist horses that struck winning form in the 1972–73 season that was, sadly, owing to Peter Cazalet's death, to be the last when the royal jumpers were trained at Fairlawne.

Fulke Walwyn succeeded as Queen Elizabeth's National Hunt trainer. He was a friend of Peter Cazalet and before having three years as a professional jockey rode as an amateur from 1929 to 1936, winning the Grand National that year on Reynoldstown. Since carrying on his training career at his yard, Saxon House Stables at Lambourn, Fulke has netted every major jumping event in the calendar, bar the Champion Hurdle. In 1981 he sent out six runners in a day that were all winners, and four weeks later produced Diamond Edge to win the Hennessy Cognac Gold Cup in November. It was the horse's first outing since winning the Whitbread Gold Cup in the previous April, and the seventh time Fulke had collected the prize since winning the inaugural race with the legendary Mandarin. And that, as the 71-year-old trainer joked, was 'not bad for someone they think is past it!' Tammuz, bred by the Queen and a half-brother to her Highclere was raced on the flat until he developed leg trouble, won the 1975 Schweppes Gold Trophy to be the biggest winner that Fulke has so far sent out for the Queen Mother. In February 1976 he saddled Sunyboy to become her 300th winner.

Game Spirit, that with The Rip headed the list in Queen Elizabeth's affections, began his racing days at Fairlawne, first a winner over hurdles and then having the initial two wins of his career as a 'chaser. In Fairlawne's last season Game Spirit was going on from strength to strength, his victory in the Whitbread Fremlins Elephant Chase, won by The Rip when the race was inaugurated, giving his owner particular pleasure.

Fulke Walwyn considers Game Spirit the best top-class horse the Queen Mother has had at Saxon House, and the horse gave him his first winner for his royal owner. In the 1974 Cheltenham Gold Cup, Game Spirit was third to the chasing giants, The Dikler and Captain Christy. In 1976 he won the Hermitage Chase after a superb dual with

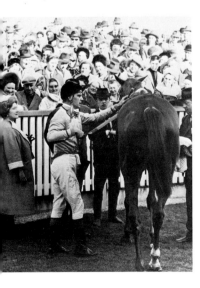

Makaldar after racing in the Champion Hurdle Challenge Cup at Cheltenham in 1967.

Bula, the ex-champion hurdler. In all he notched up 21 wins for Queen Elizabeth, but she loved him as much for his personality as for his successes. No jockey was allowed to touch Game Spirit with the whip and David Mould, who rode for the Queen Mother for many years, told the horse's rider at Newbury in 1975: '. . . if you give him a pat in the race, you'll get the same response as showing the whip to another horse.' When Game Spirit's racing career came to an end it was planned he would go to Windsor as a hack for the Queen, a role for which a horse of such character was admirably fitted but which tragically he was not to fulfil.

This horse always loved racing at Newbury, and when he beat Bula it was his ninth win on the course. A year later, in 1977, he was running there again. His jockey, Bill Smith, stable jockey at Saxon House and the present royal jockey, had no feeling during the race that there was anything seriously wrong with his horse, but was disappointed when he dropped back five fences from home to finish fifth. With the rest of the field they then went out of sight behind the stand beyond the winning post. As Bill Smith turned to leave the course Game Spirit staggered and fell dead from a massive haemorrhage of the lungs. That was a tragic day for Queen Elizabeth and a very sad one both for the racing world and the public who had taken Game Spirit, a horse that always lived up to his name, to their hearts.

At the beginning of the 1978–79 season there were six home-bred royal horses at Saxon House. Amongst them were two proven performers, the half-brothers Queen's College, by the Queen's small stallion College Green (his size due to being born a twin), out of the Queen Mother's Queen of the Isle; and Isle of Man, with the same dam but by Manicou.

Isle of Man came into training at Fairlawne in 1973. He is a big tough horse, was still a bit of a handful when he came to Saxon House as a six-year-old, and has always been a hard-pulling front-runner. When he was retired, aged 14, at the end of the 1981 season, he had 14 good wins to his name and was the rumbustious character that appealed to the racing public, and one his owner always loved to watch. He is now enjoying himself hunting in the Shires.

By the end of the 1981–82 season Queen Elizabeth had had 340 winners – a good record – but it is a sign of our inflationary times and the royal family's economical policy that only five of those wins came in that season. In the heyday of the 1970–71 season she had 23 winners, but that was when there were some 15 horses in training at Fairlawne, against the 6 or 7 normally now in training with Fulke Walwyn.

Usually the Queen Mother has about five brood mares with their foals at Sandringham. The breeding routine and annual programme for them is the same as for the Queen's and is also organised by Michael Oswald and his staff. The difference in treatment begins with the weaned foals, and stems from the fact that, unlike a racer on the flat, a jumper does not usually go into training until it is four or five, and has to be looked after during the interim. These stores are kept in Norfolk, either at West Newton where a small overflow stable is run, or with Major Eldred Wilson, or with one or two other friends who live in Norfolk. During these years of its life a young horse is broken in and ridden gently, sometimes taken out hunting, developing physically and mentally before going into training.

The main difficulty about breeding 'chasers is that probably 50 per cent or more are fillies, and they do not fit in very well in a training establishment and are not popular with trainers. Queen Elizabeth is not very lucky in this respect, and in 1982 all three foals, from the mares Heather Deep, Barbella, and Roman Meeting, the only ones to produce that year, were fillies. (The mares Manushi, a six-year-old, and the nineteen-year-old Colonia were not covered, and at four, the filly Joliette was a maiden.) Of the young horses, the three-year-old bay gelding, Army Council, that is with Captain Charles Radclyffe at Lew, could be an exciting prospect for the future. Out of Roman Meeting, he is by the famous racehorse Brigadier Gerard, whose owners gave Queen Elizabeth a free nomination as a birthday present.

The Queen Mother frequently visits the stables, working out detailed plans for each horse and as she stays at Sandringham after Christmas, like the Queen she is able to go and see her mares and foals, as well as the young horses that are with her friends who all live nearby.

In February 1982 there were seven horses in training at Lambourn. Of these, Highland Line at five years old and Lunedale at four were doing little more than learning something of the sights and noise of a racecourse. Rushill was only six, and having proved scarcely fast enough for hurdling, was put to novice chasing in the latter part of the season. Cranbourne Tower, another six-year-old that is out of the Queen's Highclere, and was a winner over hurdles, was also turned to 'chasing half-way through the season and at his age also has plenty of time to develop his abilities. Prince Charles was going to ride this horse in a hurdle race at Sandown, but unfortunately it was lame on the day.

Aged nine, Special Cargo, bought as a five-year-old at the Doncaster Bloodstock Sales in 1978, is a good 'chaser, needing 3½ miles but plagued by slight lameness. The 1981–82 season was not a good one for him – he only ran four times, but although he did not win he never ran badly.

A horse that promised so much but whose career ended in tragedy, was Sindebele, bred in New Zealand and brought to Saxon House Stables at the beginning of 1981. He was sweet natured and with splendid conformation, but as a slow maturing five-year-old was not hurried. Always ridden by the young Stuart Shillston, a lad in the yard who was still doing his two horses but as a very good rider was getting a few races, Sindebele first ran with promise in two novice hurdles. He then ran a splendid race at Lingfield to be beaten by a short head. Queen Elizabeth was delighted with the horse and, like her trainer and everyone

in the yard, was really excited about his future prospects. On February 20
1982 the horse went to Chepstow where he would be meeting the best
of the season's novices. Despite high hopes the luck was out and
on 'dead' and holding ground Sindebele damaged his shoulder and
finished unplaced.

   Fulke Walwyn is renowned for his success in getting horses
'right' again, and it was decided, with Sindebele fit and well, to run him
once more, at Cheltenham, before putting him away at the end of the
season. There were 20 runners, again the best of the novices, and early
on Sindebele and Shillston were well placed second or third. Three flights

*The Queen Mother at
Sandown Park with her
laughing horse, Special
Cargo, after winning the
Alanbrooke Memorial
Handicap Chase in March
1981.*

out the horse went to the front, ears pricked, looking certain to win or only just be beaten. The Queen Mother was not at Cheltenham that day and the race was not televised, but Mr Clotworthy, the horse's previous owner, was over from New Zealand with his family and there to have the thrill of seeing him race. They were watching as Sindebele, galloping on the flat and still two strides from the final flight of hurdles, broke his off-side fetlock joint.

That was another tragedy for all concerned, but inevitably in what is only a resumé of 35 or so years of racing, the catastrophes as well as the triumphs are, so to speak, concertinaed. During that period of time Queen Elizabeth has owned more than a hundred racehorses. Some have not made the grade and were sold, by private treaty but never by public auction, or passed on to other members of the royal family or to friends. Some became past or present brood mares. One, a handsome chestnut called Brig o' Dee, was loaned to the Metropolitan Mounted Police where, despite an aversion to the trappings of ceremonial, that precluded him from such splendid occasions as the Trooping the Colour, he worked for years as an excellent horse on street patrol. The vast majority, at the end of their racing careers, have been placed in carefully selected homes, some as hunters, some as riding horses, one or two as event horses, some as trainers' or starters' hacks, but all to live out their remaining years with enjoyment. And wherever they are Queen Elizabeth likes to be kept in touch with their well-being.

A horse that must have added a certain excitement to the Queen Mother's racing, if tinged sometimes with exasperation, is Master Andrew, given to her as an 80th birthday present by the Jockey Club. Exceptionally good looking and impeccably bred, the horse has been described as 'something of a character – when good, very very good, when bad really very naughty,' and not an easy one to train. There is no question of his courage, or ability or speed, but Master Andrew used to take exception to jumping off with the others at the start. Sometimes he whipped round, sometimes dwelt until the other horses were a couple of hundred yards ahead before deciding to join in, and then running on very well. Despite these idiosyncrasies, the horse provided Queen Elizabeth with her first winner of the 1981–82 season. He then won again, at Lingfield, after a start where he threw up his head and broke one of Bill Smith's teeth before throwing him off. They lost ten yards or so but still made up the ground. In his next race Master Andrew's lad led him into the start, but he still played up and then showed his obvious ability by coming second in a field of good novice hurdlers.

On February 10 the Queen Mother watched her gift horse running in a high-class race at Ascot. He behaved worse than usual, being left by at least 30 yards and with the field well on their way to the first flight, before getting going to finish fourth. When he returned to Ascot in April he did jump off better in quite a high-class hurdle and won from a big field by one-and-a-half lengths.

Master Andrew always runs his races out well, but as he carries his head high he is not an easy horse to ride over hurdles. In the 1982–83 season he is to go 'chasing where it is hoped the general set-up and bigger fences will induce him to drop his head and take more notice of what he is jumping.

Just as the years have made little or no difference to the Queen Mother's commitment to her public duties, so her enthusiasm, interest, and practical knowledge in and about racing remains unimpaired. Whenever possible she goes to see each runner that she has, going down to Saxon House three or four times a season and discussing racing plans for each horse with her trainer. When the Racing Calendar arrives at Clarence House, Sir Martin Gilliat, the Queen Mother's private secretary and a great racing man, marks where each of her horses has been entered. After studying this and the relative weights, the Queen Mother makes one of her several telephone calls per week to her trainer, to discuss in which race it would be in the best interests of a horse to run. A convenient date is then fixed so that if it can possibly be fitted in with her numerous public engagements, the Queen Mother can get to see her horses race – and sometimes, after a morning engagement, that can mean a great hustle to arrive in time!

Whether her horses win or whether they lose the Queen Mother loves to see them run, and usually manages to do so about 20 times in a season, regardless of the weather. In the Fairlawne days the Kentish racecourses, Folkestone, Wye, or Fontwell Park were the most convenient. Today she goes racing mostly at Sandown, Kempton, Newbury, Windsor, and the jumping meetings at Ascot and, as always, wherever she goes she is acclaimed as the most popular and sporting owner in National Hunt racing. Her trainers have always admired and acted on her considerable knowledge and accurate judgements and she is always welcomed in the yards by the stable lads with whom she has friendly chats about all the horses there. The horses look for her coming and the apples she carries in her pockets.

The many jockeys who have ridden for the Queen Mother through the years all bear witness to the concern she has for them in what is admittedly a dangerous trade and none of them ever hears a word of remonstrance, whatever happens in a race. If one is injured she never fails to write and send him books and gifts, and many years ago she became Patron of the Injured Jockeys Fund.

Apart from racing, the Queen Mother always enjoys the royal family outing to Badminton, especially if Princess Anne or Captain Phillips is competing. She goes to a number of agricultural shows and is fascinated by the Shire and working horses she sees there. She also has a very soft spot for Shetlands and was happy to become Patron of the Shetland Pony Association. But racing and racehorses are her first love and she has every possible sympathy with Prince Charles's racing aspirations.

As one of the Queen Mother's trainers once remarked: 'If she's won or if she's beaten, she's just the same. She's a real good sport.'

ABOVE LEFT: *The Queen Mother at the Badminton Horse Trials.*

ABOVE RIGHT: *Watching progress with the crowds at Badminton.*

BELOW: *The Queen Mother inspecting the course at Cheltenham.*

110

Chapter Eight

Charles: The Prince and his Horses

WHEN PRINCE CHARLES started racing over fences, the Queen Mother was one of his greatest supporters, both in spirit and once in actual presence on the day. There were to be moments when things went wrong, but she must have felt very proud on that occasion in October 1980 when her 'very special' grandson, riding at Ludlow in only the second race in his life, came past the post with his loved partner Allibar to finish a highly respectable second. And maybe her thoughts strayed back in time to Charles as a small boy grappling with this difficult art of riding, and then later faced with the little jumps at gymkhanas which he frankly admits scared him stiff.

Charles was about four or five when he first climbed on a pony and was taught the rudiments such as where to put his feet and how to hold the reins, by the Queen. He has always loved horses, and he loved that pony, particularly when standing safely on the ground beside it, but still recalls the painful difficulties of trying to learn to rise to the trot. The start of his riding career was not made any easier by seeing his sister, Anne, 16 months younger, clamouring to get on a pony as well and then taking to it like a duck to water. Only three years later, while her brother

Prince Charles on his favourite horse Allibar in the Club Amateur Riders' Handicap Steeplechase at Ludlow in October 1980.

The young Prince Charles on Greensleeves and Princess Anne on William riding at Windsor in 1957.

was rather timidly coming to terms with his pony Greensleeves, Anne was charging happily around on William, a small, lively pony with which she was most obviously 'at one'.

Charles is not the first boy to have been faced with the problem of a younger sister possessed of twice the confidence over riding he had himself, and not backward in handing out unsolicited advice. When they began attending Horace Smith's riding school and were taught by Sybil Smith, who helped instruct the Queen and Princess Margaret, the story was much the same. Charles would go happily into the stables and pet and talk to the largest horse, but was much more cautious in his approach to the actual riding than the keener, more talented Anne. Later both children joined the Garth Hunt Branch of the Pony Club and for some time, for competing purposes, shared an able little cream-coloured pony called Bandit, on loan from the Crown Equerry's sister. At the Pony Club gymkhanas they both won a number of rosettes with this very willing performer, mostly for jumping, but although Charles was not to be outdone by his sister he was still distinctly nervous, particularly of 'leaving the ground'. His riding nerve was not improved when they rode together in the park and Anne, always a speed merchant, used to hurtle by. Inevitably Charles's pony would join in and, despite pleas to his sister to stop, the gallop usually ended only where the turf ran out.

Despite his affection for Bandit, for Charles it was not altogether a sad day when, at around the age of 13, he outgrew the pony. There were by then few other boys in his branch of the Pony Club, and he felt he could no longer cope with competing. There was some attempt to find him a suitable larger animal but none of them appealed. He was by then at public school and there were plenty of other sports and hobbies to fill his leisure, both in term time and during the holidays.

For as long as he could remember, during the Easter holidays

Prince Charles and Princess Anne competing in the Ascot Gymkhana in April 1963.

and before setting off to Scotland in early August, Charles had enjoyed going with the Queen and Anne to Smith's Lawn on Sunday afternoons, to watch Prince Philip play polo. As soon as they were old enough the children used to lend a hand holding ponies between chukkas and became very attached to them, knowing each by name. As he grew older Charles became more and more engrossed with the game itself. It was fast and exciting and the rules and techniques became clearer the more he watched and asked questions. It was thrilling to hear the drumming of hooves as his father came racing down the field to ride-off an opponent. Inevitably there were bumps, bruises, and falls but Charles felt this was an invigorating and enthralling form of equitation and one in which there was not a fence in sight. When he was in his fifteenth year and Prince Philip suggested he should take up the game, Charles was all for it.

His first pony was San Quinina, loaned to him by his father. She was a small, compact Argentinian mare, not in her first youth but still handy and one who knew her job from A to Z. Well schooled and well mannered she was just the type to give her rider confidence and if she ever showed signs of becoming spoilt Prince Philip quickly straightened her out. For a time Charles hacked the mare quietly round the Home

Park at Windsor establishing mutual rapport, and used a wooden 'horse' when being instructed in the various strokes by his father. Soon he was sufficiently proficient to ride San Quinina in stick-and-ball sessions on the castle lawn with a friend of his own age, the son of Colonel Gerard Leigh, then chairman of the Household Brigade Polo Club (now the Guards Polo Club). In the Easter holidays of 1964 he played in a 'friendly' or two on the sacred turf of Smith's Lawn. Because of his youth and inexperience this idea had occasioned a few grumbles from the experts, but by then Charles had added Sombra, a gift from Lord Cowdray, to his embryonic string of polo ponies. She was a twenty-year-old even more knowledge-able about the game than San Quinina, and her new owner always thought of her as the exact equivalent of the 'Maltese Cat', the polo pony in Kipling's immortal story. The Prince does not agree with those who consider good horsemanship is not essential for playing good polo, and readily admits both his riding and his game then left much to be desired, but San Quinina and Sombra saw to it he did not disgrace them, and both old ponies taught him 'an awful lot'. By the end of that season he had achieved a handicap of − 1

In the following years Charles was ably coached by Prince Philip and his great-uncle, the late Lord Mountbatten. In 1967 there was a first success in tournament polo when playing for Windsor Park and they triumphed in the final of the low-goal Combermere Cup. His handi-cap rose to 0 at the end of that season, and a year later he was promoted to 1. The Prince played regularly for the university team while he was at Cambridge, and rose to 2 handicap. While he was in the navy he played

Prince Charles, aged fourteen, riding his pony San Quinina in a practice polo game on Smith's Lawn.

whenever the 'exigencies of the service' allowed. His handicap rose to 3 and in 1973 he made his debut in the more demanding levels of high-goal polo. A year later he played in the team which won the medium-goal Harrison Cup at Cowdray.

In February 1976 Prince Charles was given his own command, the mine-hunter *Bronington*, and as the ship was on duty in the northern approaches there were few, if any, opportunities for polo. The command was a brief one as the Prince left the navy with the rank of Lieutenant Commander, to return to civilian life and his duties as heir to the throne, in December of that year. In the following season he played high-goal polo with the Golden Eagles, and in July captained Young England against France.

By this time Charles had a new tutor, the flamboyant one-time 10-goal Australian, Sinclair Hill, the man who has had the most influence on the Prince's polo life. For two seasons the Australian, a brilliant instructor, became his mentor, and as the Prince says: '. . . revolutionised the whole thing for me – it made a total difference to my outlook and tactical approach to the game.' Sinclair Hill, a firm believer in the necessity of good riding in order to play good polo, also improved Prince Charles's horsemanship. He himself is convinced he could never have achieved his present position, now firmly established amongst the twenty best English players, if he had not learned to control his pony, using it as a vehicle, and so be able to get on with the game without having to worry about whether he could start or stop as required.

Nowadays the Australian does not visit England so often but when he does and even if he is merely a spectator in the crowd, Charles finds himself inspired to try to impress him by playing extra well.

For a while after he first began playing polo, the Prince was worried about his riding, concerned about his play and lack of experience, but he soon gained confidence. Now he can say with conviction that the original appeal of the game grows stronger each season. On his visits abroad in his official capacity he can sometimes fit in a game of polo, and he has played in many lands, including Brazil, India, America, Australia, New Zealand, Malta, and Ghana. Wherever he is, he enjoys the game that combines his love of horses with the exercise he finds a necessity of life. It provides him with both excitement and a challenge and is the one team game he can play. It says much for his determination that he has made his present handicap of 4. Of all games polo requires a great deal of time for practice and Prince Charles's time is in very short supply, like that of his father.

One facet of world-class polo-playing that the Prince is unlikely to acquire is the aggressiveness, the ruthless subjection of everything to the demands of the game that so often makes the champion. Charles has the rapport with his ponies essential for success whatever the game or sport, but his feelings for all the horses he rides go beyond this. He looks on them as friends and finds himself incapable of pushing any of them to the limit or treating them 'as a bicycle'. The Prince calls this a 'failing – if perhaps a peculiarly British one', and considers it the reason why he 'can't be *really* good at anything in the horse world. . . .' But that is an over-modest assessment of his abilities, and whether he realises it or not his 'shortcoming' is the hallmark of the real horseman.

There has always been a small proportion of home-bred ponies amongst the string Prince Charles keeps in one of the courts in the Windsor Mews. In 1979 three of them had been bred by the Queen, but to set himself up at the start of his road to playing high-goal polo, five were bought from the Argentine. Today, amongst the trained ponies he still has three Argentinian mares, one of them a gift from the captain of the Maple Leaves, a team for which the Prince plays. Another was given to him some years ago by Peter Palumbo, a well known player now retired who lives near Windsor, and for the 1982 season loaned him Willie, a very good white pony (technically a grey). Now, from choice and also in the interest of economy, all the other ponies are home-bred. The majority are out of Carnarita, a mare that came from Archie David, and are by the Queen's polo pony stallion standing in Gloucestershire, Sanbal, given to the Queen by Sir John Galvin. On his dam's side Sanbal is a grandson of the late Aga Khan's Derby winner, Tulyer. Before going to stud Sanbal won a number of sprints in Ireland, and since he is by

Prince Charles in fierce competition for the ball in a match at Windsor.

Palestine, an extremely fast sprinter, his progeny possess an abundance of the speed polo demands.

In 1981 Prince Charles was excited by the potential of Happiness, a young pony playing her first season, that he and the expert who brought her on considered might be as brilliant as her dam, once the champion playing mare in the Argentine and on one occasion played by Prince Philip. As highly strung as most of her kind, Happiness was at first inclined to get up on her hind legs and had to be ridden with great tact. (Prince Philip used to say that if he made rude remarks to Betaway she would demonstrate her annoyance by rearing!) But Happiness began to settle down and by July 1981 Prince Charles was able to play her in an international match, where her handiness and speed exceeded his highest hopes. Then the mare went lame only a quarter of the way through the season which was bad luck because the Prince is always careful to remember not to 'over-do it' – a point that is easily overlooked with a potentially brilliant young pony. It is such a joy to handle that the player starts to feel he can go straight into 22-goal polo which, if done too early in a pony's career, can put it off and wreck it for life.

Amongst Prince Charles's string of high quality ponies, Pan's Folly won the Vickers Cup for the best heavyweight pony in 1979, and Carnival is another of his 'specials'. He says he can do anything on her, and makes the point that a good pony like this, one that is marvellous to handle and ride, can put a player's handicap up by another goal. The player can concentrate entirely on the game and such ponies make it easy to hit the ball because they go straight.

Mayfair, still only partly trained in 1981, is one the Queen finds especially interesting as she was sired by Sanbal, and is a granddaughter of Mayerling, a mare played by Prince Philip that came originally from Lord Mountbatten. The home-bred Sapper, another of the younger ones, is out of Pecas, the skewbald Argentine mare given to Prince Charles by the Royal Warrant Holders Association as a present to mark his 21st birthday.

The Prince has an expert to make his ponies but, as his father discovered when he was playing, those who really know the job do not grow on trees. There are not many people in England with the ability and the demand for those who have it well exceeds the supply. The rising costs of bringing made ponies over from the Argentine was becoming prohibitive, even before the invasion of the Falklands made it impossible. Yet, despite the economic climate of today when the expenses of high-goal polo would seem to exclude all but the few, sponsorship has ensured that more people are playing, with more teams in the high-goal tournaments than ever before. Polo is also growing in popularity with riding clubs and is an up-and-coming game at the Pony Club grass-roots. Pony Club polo tournaments were started at Aldershot in 1958, and in 1981 the annual championships played at Cowdray Park over three days attracted a total of 30 teams. It would seem that the future of polo is assured.

In addition to the help received with his riding from Sinclair

Royal Horses

Hill, Prince Charles's horsemanship, and in turn his polo-playing, has benefited enormously from the various other forms of equitation he has taken up in the past few years. He has always been one to try out as many different aspects as possible of each sport he takes up and ever since he was a boy it had rankled that basically he was still scared of jumping. To overcome this 'silly, irrational' fear was a challenge that became a 'must'. The Prince believes that facing physical challenges greatly improves the ability to meet with success the much harder mental and spiritual ones, a philosophy underlying the more hazardous undertakings in which he has been involved.

In this case, about seven years ago the Prince decided to enlist Princess Anne's help in learning to jump, a skill that as European Individual Eventing Champion she was eminently qualified to teach! Charles has a well tried theory – one that must be every teacher's most fervent, if rarely fulfilled prayer – that in order to be taught anything it is necessary to wipe all preconceived notions from your mind and accept that your instructor really does know considerably more about the matter in hand than you do. And as perhaps the most important adjunct to this successful instructor/pupil relationship, the Princess, who is an excellent judge of a horse's character, hit on exactly the right animal to fit the situation. Had she not chosen so wisely, her brother reckons he would not have been involved in the various sports embracing jumping that he has since tried out.

The horse was Pinkers, a cob loaned by Mrs Phillips, Princess Anne's mother-in-law, his name a reflection of his unusual strawberry-roan colouring. According to the Prince, his looks were more 'incredible' than conventionally handsome, but he was exactly what was needed to give his rider confidence. Pinkers jumped beautifully, never stopped unless required, choosing his own pace for coming into fences without pulling or going too fast, and took care of his rider whatever happened. He had come originally from the Ledbury country, and after partnering Prince Charles in some successful jumping tuition, also provided the perfect answer as the hunter for trying out the sport that followed.

The Prince has never forgotten the interest and excitement he felt as a child when taken to a meet of the West Norfolk Hunt, and for the first time saw hounds and heard the notes of a hunting horn. Since then, hunting had remained in the back of his mind as something he wished to experience, but had never done, partly because of the feeling against the sport by a relatively small proportion of the community, but chiefly because of his anxieties over jumping. With that fear then behind him, he decided to find out for himself what hunting was all about.

The Duke of Beaufort, then the Master of the Horse and Master of the Beaufort Hounds, arranged a private meet at Badminton. Fortified by a try out with Princess Anne the previous evening over a few fences of the Beaufort country, and safely if not entirely conventionally clad, Prince Charles set out on a day of discovery with the experienced Pinkers.

120

Since that day in 1975, of drenching rain, of a five-mile 'point' and the exhilaration of jumping in the first flight everything that came, the Prince has hunted with 42 different packs all over Britain. But like most who hunt he knows it is little good trying to explain to the uninitiated why he does it. It is not that an explanation is impossible because the sport is 'indefensible', but because hunting is compounded of such an indescribable mixture of scents and sounds and other country aspects, of attitudes to conservation and what it really means, of talk with real country people, all combined with a spice of danger and the sheer thrill of riding across unknown country. That and so much more can only be appreciated by those who sample hunting for themselves – as was discovered by a somewhat 'anti' journalist who, before writing a book against the sport felt he should take up hunting and 'see for himself', and then wrote a reasoned treatise in favour.

Prince Charles with the Quorn Hunt on November 15 1980.

Prince Charles, a sensitive man, understands the depth of feeling of many of those who oppose hunting, but wishes they really understood the horrors of the other methods of the control that is necessary, because in Britain there is now no natural predator capable of keeping the fox population within bounds. Foxes are notoriously hard to shoot and, since they do not lick their wounds to cleanse them, a single pellet usually means an agonisingly slow death from gangrene; anyone who has come

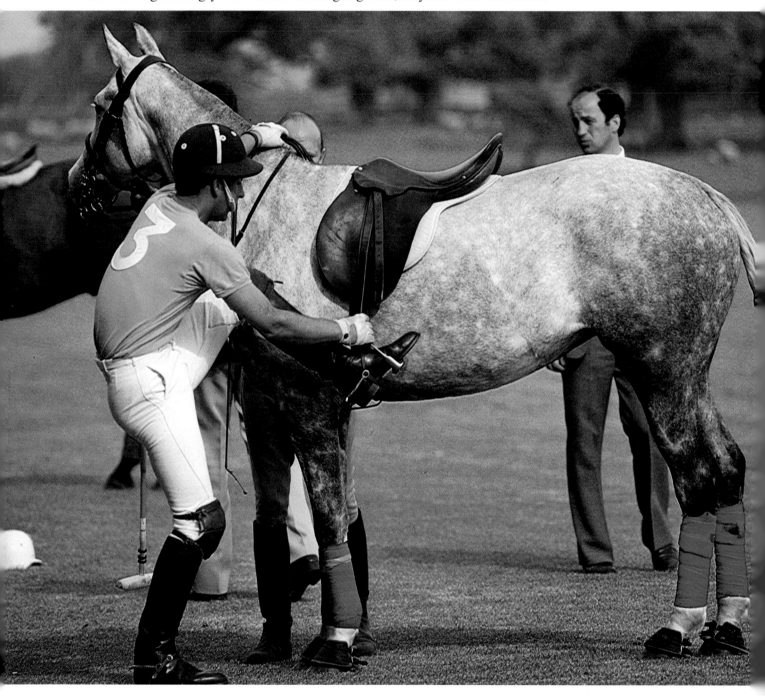

LEFT: *Prince Charles mounts his pony before a polo game in Oxfordshire.*

RIGHT: *Prince Charles passing villagers on his way from the Cheshire Hunt.*

across a fox killed by poison cannot fail to realise the appalling suffering of that death; a fox trapped in a snare not regularly visited, starves to death or bites off a limb in order to escape; even the gassing, recommended for years by the Ministry of Agriculture for exterminating badgers suspected of infecting cattle with tuberculosis, is now shown to cause much suffering.

Like so many who hunt, Prince Charles, while accepting the necessity, takes no pleasure in the prospect of a kill and is always glad on the many occasions when the fox gets away. If it evades hounds it is 'an all right' fox, if it does not it is a dead one, but at least it is not maimed.

For the Prince hunting first of all provides a marvellous way of seeing rural Britain and meeting people, farmers, locals, 'ordinary British blokes', that would not otherwise be possible. He claims that while out hunting with many different packs, he has visited remote 'backs of beyond', be it in Northumberland, or in Wales, or the Shires, that he would otherwise never have known existed. He acknowledges that there is a grain of truth in the concept of hunting as an elitist, upper-class sport. There are people like that who hunt but the majority are not and he himself has met people from more different walks of life when out hunting than in the case of any other sport.

To some extent hunting is a risky business and for Charles that is part of its attraction, and part of its justification. He feels the dice is equally loaded for both the hunter and the hunted and maintains that open gateways are no alternative to taking a straight line across the country. Here is an opportunity to face up to a challenge and it is one up to the fox if the horse you are riding fails to notice the ditch on the far side of a hairy fence. He has had a number of spectacular falls, occasionally more than one in a day, and including the time when 'like a fool' he jumped into the middle of an unsuspected bog. Not surprisingly his horse turned a somersault and its rider dived in head first, to re-emerge plastered in mud and bloody nosed, but quite unbowed. As with polo or racing or any other strenuous form of equitation, he reckons a fall is an accepted part of the business. But apart from his determination to ride in a straight line without the benefit of gates or gaps, Prince Charles does not court disaster. For him, one aspect of a good day with hounds is 'the thrill of trying to get across country in one piece'. People hunt for a variety of reasons – some principally because they enjoy watching hounds working, and to them the Prince 'hunts to ride'. But on a blank day when nothing much happens and the galloping and jumping is minimal or non-existent, he 'still loves being out . . .', and that is the enjoyment of a countryman.

Sadly the admirable Pinkers died in the summer of 1976, and since then Prince Charles has hunted a number of different horses, each providing a different facet to his enjoyment of the day, each adding to the experience that has made him an accomplished horseman. Often his horse has been provided by Sir John Miller, or by his host for the day's hunting, and although riding a strange horse can be quite anxious work Prince Charles has crossed some of the most strongly fenced hunting countries – always at the front of the field. 'The horse is a great leveller', as Prince Philip discovered. Yet in the heat of the chase there is never any question of exerting royal protocol at a fence, and no-one could set a better example of coolness, courage, and genuine interest, not to mention good manners which some who have hunted for many more years would do well to mirror.

For the 1981–82 season the Prince was loaned an ex-'chaser, whose marvellous flair for 'going at his fences' when he sees them has convinced his rider that the next steeplechaser he acquires must have this same trait. Another hunter for which Charles had the greatest affection is Candlewick, a 17-hand brown mare belonging to the Queen. A half-sister to Columbus, Candlewick was originally ridden by Princess Anne and began competing in novice one-day events in the autumn of 1975. Unfortunately in 1976, on an obscure novice course in Dorset, the mare hit the top of a fence, catapulted the Princess on to the rock hard ground and fell on top of her. Although later the Princess was to insist 'it wasn't too drastic . . . it was muscle more than bone damage . . .', she was badly concussed and bruised. Candlewick was also very stiff and sore after the fall, and was turned out for a while at Hampton Court with Columbus, recovering from a leg injury.

Nothing like that occurred when Prince Charles was hunting the mare and he established a wonderful relationship with her. She had been beautifully schooled by Alison Oliver, who helped Princess Anne with her horses until her marriage, but although her manners made her a joy to ride, like many mares Candlewick could be temperamental. When they got going on a good run – and after a mile or so she was well warmed up – she was unbeatable and, according to Lord Oaksey, 'one of the two best cross-country horses' he ever saw, but the Prince never quite knew what to expect. On another day Candlewick could be nappy, refusing to have anything to do with a hedge or something she could not see through. Having since learned something of the condition known as azoturea that spasmodically affects the muscles of the back and loins of so many horses today, the Prince feels that could have been the problem.

Eventually Candlewick went to Hampton Court as a brood mare, but there is another horse belonging to the Queen that rather un-expectedly turned out to be an exceptional hunter for Prince Charles. This is the redoubtable Mexico, the other one of Lord Oaksey's best 'cross-country horses'. He has no great speed, but that is understandable as he was bought in Sweden by the Crown Equerry as a royal carriage horse and was driven by Prince Philip in the World Driving Championships. When it came to jumping in or out of the hunting field Mexico is as bold and agile as any Prince Charles has ridden.

Hunting not only removed the last remnant of the Prince's anxiety about jumping, it also taught him there are few more thrilling experiences than jumping fences at speed across country on a good horse. The progression to the then quite new sport of team-jumping across country seemed only natural.

Chapter Nine

Competition Riding

PRINCE CHARLES rode Mexico in his first team cross-country, at the Vale of the White Horse event in 1978. This was only four years after the sport had been dreamed up by Douglas Bunn at Hickstead, as a spin-off to the world famous All-England Jumping Course he inaugurated there in 1960. The first event had caused something of a sensation, despite some forbidding falls and forecasts to the contrary, being much enjoyed by both participants and spectators, and popular on television. The following year the weather did its worst, including a fall of snow that many thought must lead to cancellation, but it was proved that this sport, like hunting, could go ahead under almost any conditions except hard frost. It encouraged other organisations, especially the hunts, to run cross-country team events for themselves which quickly became an established and enjoyable sport.

Inevitably there were some teething troubles and where originally, apart from some basics, the aim was to avoid rules and regulations, necessary advice and guide-lines are now obtainable. The chief essential is a course-builder who has himself galloped a horse across country over fences. He then knows from experience the capability of a horse and will utilise wherever possible natural hedges and posts-and-rails, avoiding small island fences and narrow trappy ones.

The emphasis in this sport is on the team aspect. Prince Charles rode as an ordinary member of his team, accepting and carrying out any instructions to the letter. This meant walking the course on the day and concerned such matters as choosing the shortest route possible, without taking undue risks that could stop them getting round, the safest take-off spots, and the optimum pace for the state of the ground and conditions. The sport is confined to two half seasons a year, one in the spring and the other in the autumn. By 1981 the Prince had competed with his team in five half-seasons during which they had two wins, several placings and one disqualification. It was typical that on Charles's first try-out he turned down the suggestion that the team should treat it as a 'school', and insisted on going 'for real'. In that first half-season he rode with the dash and verve that showed him well able to hold his own with the best, and proved the point on the occasion of his team's first victory. Having seen one of his group fall at the fourth fence the Prince realised his own score must count (there are four riders to a team but only the three best scores

Prince Charles rides Collingwood in a cross-country team event in the Cotswolds.

are taken), and rode like one inspired over the remaining 20 fences, finishing only a few lengths behind the leader.

Sometimes he was loaned horses for these cross-country events, sometimes he rode his own. After introducing Candlewick to the sport he was given a telling illustration of the mare's temperamental nature. The first time she obviously enjoyed herself and went 'like a bomb', but on her second outing her lack of enthusiasm had already left them well adrift by the third fence. At the seventh, a flight of rails, she packed it in. Disregarding the limelight in which the Prince of Wales inevitably has to compete, anyone who has suffered the exasperation and embarrassment of fighting a losing battle with a horse in that frame of mind, can well understand why Candlewick was temporarily downgraded from being 'favourite horse'.

This is another sport in which falls are an accepted part of the game and the Prince collected his share, although he only counted one as being a real 'humdinger'. The most annoying was at the Warwickshire event when he was riding in his customary position of third man. By the fifteenth fence his team, that day the Earl of Chester's Chasers (named from one of his titles), looked assured of victory, but then disaster struck when the Prince and a team-mate collided to bring each other down at the water. Apart from putting the team out of the running, this fall posed a problem of identification for the officials, watching through binoculars. Both riders were mounted on greys, both were sodden and covered in mud – and although an irrelevancy, both are said to have been making much the same remarks!

The grey Prince Charles was riding that day was Collingwood, loaned him on several occasions for these events, and the horse with which he had success and the most fun. Apart from Collingwood's ability there were family reasons why the Prince should be interested in riding him. The horse was another bred by the Queen, a younger but full brother to Columbus. Both were out of Trim Ann and sired by Colonist, a tough old customer that stood at Sandringham and was once a successful 'chaser belonging to Sir Winston Churchill.

Princess Anne was schooling Collingwood and Columbus at the time she was forming her successful partnership with Doublet. The two greys were then both young and green, but although she felt Collingwood was upgraded too quickly, by the autumn of 1971 she was riding both in Intermediate events. The younger grey jumped well, particularly over show fences for his stage of training, but in those days lacked Columbus's boldness across country. He was always a sweet-natured horse that tried hard, but by the spring of 1972 had grown to his full strength and was a bit of a handful. Lack of time forced Anne to dispense with one of them and since Columbus, if very strong and impetuous, was by then displaying great potential, Collingwood was passed on to another home. Like his half-sister Candlewick, Collingwood's schooling had been undertaken by Princess Anne and Alison Oliver, and Prince Charles found him equally well mannered and with the courage time had brought to match his innate jumping ability.

Lady Diana with Nick Gasalee, who trains Good Prospect for Prince Charles, at Sandown in the spring of 1981.

The Prince's enjoyable team events had to come to an end through lack of time when another, even more challenging sport became a possibility. His participation had helped popularise competitive cross-country riding and he himself had gained a lot of very useful experience. It had been a natural progression from hunting, just as steeplechasing was to be a natural progression from the team events, but whereas he continues to enjoy his hunting, the other had to be sacrificed with the advent of 'chasing.

Racing, over fences and as a participant rather than a spectator, had been another of Charles's apparently unattainable dreams. The confidence he gained from hunting and the even faster galloping over fences in a team, brought his dream into the realms of possibility, and the world of National Hunt racing welcomed the idea with enthusiasm. He chose Nick Gaselee as his trainer, an ex-amateur steeplechase jockey whose yard is at Lambourn, near that of the Queen Mother's trainer, Fulke Walwyn. Then, while Prince Charles began acquiring something of the art of a jockey in the very limited time at his disposal, Nick Gaselee searched for a suitable horse for the heir to the throne to race.

Of course, it had to be a good horse, and also a smooth jumper, reasonably safe, and capable of winning without the force and expertise of an experienced, professional jockey. All horses have a will of their own and even the most compliant racer may not always respond to the braking and steering wishes of its jockey, but this one must not be in any way 'bloody minded'. There proved to be an answer to this problem in the form of Allibar, a ten-year-old bought in Ireland and chosen with the aid of a member of the British Bloodstock Agency. It was an excellent buy. Allibar was an honest horse that knew his job, had won in good company, and came second in his first English outing, at Worcester, ridden by Richard Linley.

In the meantime and with the Queen Mother to cheer him on, Prince Charles had his first ride over fences at Sandown in very heavy going. He was riding a chestnut called Sea Swell and although finishing fourth out of five, had survived a couple of jumping blunders and jumped clear over an admittedly tricky course. It was an encouraging start.

The plan was for the Prince and Allibar to have one race in public in the autumn, that three-mile Amateur Riders' 'Chase at Ludlow in which they went so well, and then to have a season of hunter 'chases and amateur riders' races, beginning at the Newbury meeting in February 1981. This would give Prince Charles a definite season for fitness, a three-month period to aim for, and fitness, even for someone who has always been 'mad about exercise' and says he cannot exist without it, was or could have been a problem. He walks and swims whenever possible and tends to run up and down long flights of stairs in preference to taking the lift – as his staff know to their cost. Polo helps keep him fit in early summer, in winter the occasional day out with hounds helps to do the same. He keeps his weight down and fortunately, as he says, 'still bounce when I fall'. For a man in public life the Prince keeps himself remarkably fit. But that is not necessarily racing fit, and as every trainer knows the only way to get really fit for race-riding, is by frequently riding in races – something the Prince of Wales, with little time even to train and ride work, cannot do. Perhaps only the other amateur jockeys against whom he raced could really appreciate the difficulties with which Prince Charles was faced at the start of his racing career. As amateurs, no doubt they all had other commitments, but most likely these were connected with horses, soldiering, farming, or some activity from which it is possible to take reasonable time off to ride work and race more than occasionally. The majority would also have had years of point-to-pointing behind them in which to gain experience and learn the trade. The Prince's public life leaves him very little time for anything as demanding as race-riding, and it says much for his interest and determination that, like his horse he was fit and well ready to run by the second week in February. Since Christmas he had set about toning up the special muscles used in steeplechasing, by every recommended means apart from actual racing. He had religiously done all the scheduled exercises daily, whenever possible rode a bicycle, with seat off the saddle, and considers his usual few days ski-ing in Switzerland helped. He had also got to know Allibar really well in their relatively few training sessions.

Charles making good progress on Candlewick in a cross-country team event at Cirencester.

They had struck up an excellent relationship and when he says: 'I really loved that horse. He just suited me perfectly,' that is the simple truth. In that first and, as fate decreed, only race together, the horse had made it plain he knew exactly what he was about. Afterwards, when asked about that happy experience Prince Charles described it as: 'A marvellous thrill, as exciting as anything I've ever done!' But he gave Allibar the credit. 'He was such a wonderful old horse . . . it was entirely due to him, nothing to do with me. When I thought I saw where I wanted to jump, he said: "No, I know what I'm doing . . .!" and he got me over all of them!'

Right from the start the Grand Military Gold Cup, run at Sandown in March, had been the target, but a scheduled preliminary race at the Newbury meeting in February was frosted off. The next date was to be the Cavalry Hunters' Chase at Chepstow on February 21.

On the previous day, three days before the public announcement of their engagement, Lady Diana went with Prince Charles to watch him give Allibar a pre-race workout on the Lambourn gallops. It was a six-furlong canter and the horse went very well. Happy and satisfied, the Prince was walking him back when Allibar began to buckle at the knees and Nick Gaselee shouted to his rider to get off. As he jumped clear the

Prince Charles competing in a North Warwickshire Hunt team cross-country event.

horse collapsed and rolled over, dead of a ruptured aorta, the main artery under the heart.

Lady Diana had been with Judy Gaselee watching the training session from a Land Rover. She ran across to Charles and it is not difficult to understand their shared distress. To lose any pet is bad enough, but there is a special relationship with a dog or horse that makes it that much worse. The Prince has always had a romantic idea about achieving a complete partnership with a horse. It was a dream, then lying shattered at his feet, that he had felt was fast materialising.

The only fortunate thing was that the horse's heart gave up then, and not taking a fence when racing. Since that day there have been rumours of a brutally hard race Allibar won in Ireland the year before the Prince bought him. A gallant horse being beaten up the straight, beyond his limit, could have strained his heart, but no-one can tell if that was the reason. It makes no difference to the tragedy when it occurs, but calamities like that are a part of the racing scene as Queen Elizabeth the Queen Mother knows only too well.

Allibar's loss might have made Prince Charles decide to give up or postpone his racing ambitions, but by training and philosophy he has been steeled to pick himself up and carry on. He might even have felt he owed it to Allibar to continue, but whatever his other reasons he wanted to bring those hard weeks of preparation to fulfilment and ride as intended in the Grand Military. That left three weeks in which to find and get to know a suitable horse.

Finding the substitute was Nick Gaselee's daunting job. The time of year was against him, at that stage of the season few trainers would be selling a good horse. The one Irish prospect he had in mind fell through, and then he thought of Good Prospect. The little horse, a year older than Allibar and higher class, had a very good reputation in amateur contests. He had been a good staying hurdler who converted readily to fences, and had won five handicap steeplechases in the previous season. It was helpful that Gaselee had seen Good Prospect, ridden by an amateur, run very well in a three-mile 'chase to be beaten by a short head. To buy this horse seemed a good gamble and anyway there were no other options.

The new purchase was good-looking, known to be a battler and able to act on any ground except the very heavy. In some ways he was an easier ride than Allibar, who took a very strong hold whether he was racing or not, but both physically and mentally Good Prospect was a very different type of horse. Prince Charles was used to Allibar's comfortingly 'good front' conformation that the new, smaller horse lacked, and he must have had the feeling it might be only too easy to 'pitch over the handlebars'. Then time was not on their side. Even when the Prince started race-training, time was in such short supply a deliberate gamble had been taken in denying him the usual wider experience of riding different animals. Under the circumstances it had been a legitimate risk to let him get used only to Allibar. Now, with the race almost upon them, and without in effect ever having ridden more than one 'chaser, he was trying to adjust to an animal with an unfamiliar style of jumping, and one that did not 'take his rider round'. Good Prospect was able and willing but he had to be ridden into his fences, tending to slow a little as he came in and 'putting in a quick one' if asked to stand off. There was none of that marvellous sensation of flying fences the Prince had known with Allibar – and was to experience when hunting a loaned ex-chaser. And when Good Prospect clipped the top of a fence, as he was prone to do, or things went a little more wrong, he was not an easy horse to sit – as Prince Charles later discovered, two experienced jockeys had already found this out for themselves.

On March 13 the Prince lined up Good Prospect for the start of the Military Gold Cup at Sandown, with over three miles and 22 fences in front of them and the daunting, or maybe stimulating knowledge that he had been made favourite by the bookies. By the eleventh fence they were still close up, then lost their position and dropped back, but were soon making up ground so fast Nick Gaselee was convinced they would win. They were lying sixth when Good Prospect blundered badly at the eighteenth fence and unseated his rider.

Some people suggested the fall might put Charles off steeple-chasing, but obviously they did not know their man. Disappointed, angry with himself, but still enthusiastic and keen to keep going, he rode at Cheltenham the next week and, sadly, once again things went a little wrong. Good Prospect made another bad mistake, this time at the tenth, and the Prince had his second fall in five days.

LEFT: *Good Prospect.*

RIGHT: *Prince Charles on Good Prospect taking one of the early fences in fine style before his fall at the eighteenth at Sandown in March 1981.*

It was not his fault. It was the ill luck of a rider who is perforce a novice, having to acquire an unknown horse at short notice, and few experienced riders would have survived such jumping blunders on a horse with 'little in front'. Good Prospect is a good horse but as Prince Charles says: 'I haven't had enough experience to know how to deal with a horse like that, I don't sit back enough. At the beginning I was told always to try and keep off the horse's back. . . .' He came to feel it was almost a crime to let his backside even touch the saddle but, having watched a lot of jockeys since, he has come to realise that he must sit down a bit more over a fence. He has also come to the conclusion that he likes a horse that takes a hold. In the early days with Allibar he was a little worried by the horse's pulling, but as they grew mutually confident he came to like it, and now realises that with a horse like that he can sit back a bit and get his feet out into a better, stronger position for tackling a fence.

That second fall was, literally a crashing disappointment. It was not helped by the inescapable headlines and public discussion as to whether the heir to the throne should or should not continue to take the risks inherent in such a sport as steeplechasing. Accustomed as he is to the relentless publicity, as is only to be expected where the royal family life is concerned, Prince Charles still finds it unbelievable that people should make such a fuss when he has a fall. When he had one playing polo in Australia the attention it received made him feel 'an absolute idiot!'

But although he naturally enjoys any sport more when he is doing it well, even as things turned out he really loved those rides. Apart from the pleasure of the actual racing, he enjoyed and appreciated the whole atmosphere of the weighing-in room, the welcome and friendliness he received from the other jockeys. And as he rightly says: 'It is a whole new world you can never know unless you share a few of the risks. . . .' He also feels racing is especially British and, unlike polo and to some extent hunting, a sport not thought of as an exclusively upper-class exercise. Hand in glove with the enjoyment in the actual racing goes the fear he candidly admits he feels before the start. But in an odd kind of a way he thinks it 'a marvellous thing to be frightened, a wonderful feeling to have real adrenalin rushing round the system' – the corollary to his philosophy that: 'It's very good for one to try and overcome these fears.'

On the public attitude to his racing falls, or mishaps in any of his other sports, the Prince shares much of Princess Anne's view – that in a funny sort of way people half want them to make fools of themselves, while assuming at the same time that they should, somehow, be good at everything at the first attempt, and always automatically succeed. The racing world knows very well that for any ordinary amateur a fall in the third and fourth races of his career would be normal setbacks, important only for the lessons to be learned from them. But as the Prince of Wales is not for the general public an 'ordinary amateur', there were two main sides to the discussions about his racing misfortunes.

Prince Charles rewards his horse with sugar lumps after competing in a Quorn Hunt cross-country event.

The first concerned that peculiar idea of being 'automatically successful'. ('He's the Prince of Wales, isn't he?' Lesser mortals may need years of experience and practice but not he – 'he's royalty, he should be able to do it!') The other argument came from the 'safety-first-at-all-costs' brigade, who regard steeplechasing as a dangerous pastime with risks to which the heir to the throne should not be exposed. There are risks in National Hunt racing, just as there are in flying aeroplanes and helicopters, in parachuting, ski-ing, skin-diving under the Arctic ice or going down 60 feet underwater to the wreck of the Mary Rose, all pastimes enjoyed by Prince Charles when the opportunity has arisen.

As the Queen has observed, it is possible to fall out of bed and break a leg. She has always understood the need for her husband and family to relieve the pressures and restrictions of royal life and constant publicity with, often, violent exercise, and appreciates their view that a spot of danger adds spice to the sports involved. The royal family are not 'fussers', and in pursuit of their various sports and pastimes share the Queen's philosophy – to take any sensible precautions and then get on with the enjoyment.

The Prince admits he has found steeplechasing more difficult than he had imagined, that the many skills attached to it are so specialised there is a great deal more to it than the, not always easy, ability to sit a galloping horse over fences. But experience can only be gained with practice, and he has a plentiful supply of requisite 'guts'. As the headlines and debates faded out of the news, Prince Charles went down to Newton Abbot and rode round hurdles on his grandmother's Upton Grey.

On one occasion the Prince drove a harness-racer, relative to the sport that despite the National Harness Racing Club is little known in southern Britain but has been adopted by America as her own. Seated in the saddle of the fragile-looking sulky, that calls for a balanced if some-what precarious position of wide-stretched legs and feet thrust into stirrups – leaving a small but unattractively gaping void between driver and the back end of his horse – the Prince set out on his voyage of discovery. History does not relate what he thought of it but since he was driving a pacer, once the mare got going he will have experienced that exhilarating sensation of speed and power when the horse rolls forward into its stride, legs moving smoothly like pistons, and the wind whips past as though one is doing a ton up!

Pacers, banned on the Continent where France's 'le trotteur' reigns supreme, employ a gait that with the American Standard Bred is partly in-bred, but always aided by the hopples (or hobbles) round its legs that are regulation racing leg-harness. The pacers are then in fact using the same gait as a camel, as Prince Charles may or may not have known when he embarked on riding one during a hilarious 'jolly' in aid of charity, in the annual Christmas show at Olympia. Based on this experience his only recorded comment about camels is that: 'They emit the most foul-smelling air at both ends!'

The highly competitive and specialised world of professional show-jumping is not one Prince Charles is ever likely to explore but in 1981, for fun and in the excellent cause of fund-raising for charity, he had a go at those highly coloured fences. This was at Ascot, competing in aid of the Racing Industry's contribution to the Year of the Disabled. He was partnered by Frisbee, belonging to the King's Troop, as famous for their impeccable ceremonial and firing royal salutes as for the breathtaking musical drive when six-horse gun teams drawing the heavy, rattling limbers criss-cross each other at the gallop with split-second timing. The Troop have also for years made their mark competitively, particularly in one and three-day eventing, and the Prince found Frisbee an excellent partner in jumping as many fences as possible within a given time. He rode in a similar 'joke' competition for charity at Olympia, with a horse belonging to the former show-jumper, Ted Edgar. Jet Lag is one of show-jumping's top-notchers and Charles was amazed by the way he could turn on sixpence, cutting the corners with a finesse and fencing at a speed that had little to do with his rider. It was an exciting experience and the Prince was annoyed with himself when, trying to 'place' Jet Lag at a fence, he misjudged the stride and they hit it.

Despite the other horse commitments the Prince does occasionally find time for hacking. When the bad weather after Christmas in 1981 precluded much else, he had some most enjoyable rides round the estate at Sandringham with a horse he had never ridden before, and not really contemplated as being within his orbit. This was the redoubtable Columbus, brought on by Princess Anne who found him a bit strong, and the horse Mark Phillips considered the 'best he had ever ridden' after winning Badminton together. It was also the horse that became more or less a 'cert' for the Olympic team until a slipped ligament put paid to his eventing days. There was a time when, despite Mark's denials, Columbus was so impetuous across country he was labled 'dangerous', and there has always been a kind of aura surrounding him of being more than 'a bit of a handful'. (His habit when young of jumping up and down, teeth bared, ears flattened, at the sight of a stranger near his box, may have helped foster this reputation!) So it was with a little trepidation that Prince Charles set off for his first ride on Columbus.

He found him 'marvellous', at 17 still taking a hold when he felt like it, but a real gentleman with good manners. They quickly combined, Charles thoroughly appreciative of the long stride and how, beautifully schooled, the horse would walk quietly on until, with the lightest aid, would quicken to trot or canter. A 'click' was enough to make him really go. There are some jumps in the Sandringham woods and after one fence Columbus would be off looking for the next, his powerful, clever jumping making him a joy to ride. The Prince even took him out for half a day with the West Norfolk Hounds. That is country where fences are few and far between, but they ran into someone's park and Prince Charles and Columbus had the thrill of leading the field over a line of posts-and-rails.

The Prince sold Good Prospect early in 1982. In some ways it was a sad decision, but apart from his incompatability with this

horse, racing would anyway have had to go into abeyance for a while. Prince Charles was a married man and there was a baby on the way. It was not the moment for leaving at dawn for a training gallop or rushing off to race-meetings, but it does not mean the 'chasing dream is over. Given the chance of the right horse at a 'sensible' price, the Prince hopes to start again.

Polo of course remains one of his chief recreational joys, and is a game the Princess of Wales understands and enjoys watching. Given the time there are many other facets of the horse world the Prince would like to try. He might have given some thought to eventing, but is well aware that proficiency in that first important phase, the dressage, is only attained through hours of patient schooling of both horse and rider. In many ways he would love to have the knowledge to bring on his own horses, learning how to make his own polo ponies, schooling his own hunters, but the time factor rules out any such dream. He has to have a made horse that he can get on and ride in whatever sport is the order of the day. His best loved home is in the country, but his work lies in London, and in winter only the odd occasion can be given up to racing or hunting. To justify to himself the time spent coming to Windsor to play polo at weekends during the season, he works in the car on the drive there and back.

Sometimes Prince Charles thinks he should concentrate on only one sport or game, but he does enjoy trying the different facets – and why not? By 1982 he and the Princess had acquired a new horse interest.

Amongst their wedding presents were two that Charles up to then had not been able to utilise. They were nominations to different stallions, but as Candlewick belongs to the Queen and was already at stud and the Prince had no suitable mare of his own, he had been unable to avail himself of the offers. Then he heard that a filly with wonderful 'chasing blood in her veins was for sale, and bought her. She is out of a mare called Indamanda and one of the last sired by Spartan General, the same grand stallion that belonged to the late John Thorne and sired Spartan Missile, second in the 1980 Grand National when ridden by his gallant owner. The filly foaled in April and the Prince then sent her to Renezzo, one of the nominated stallions. The hope is to breed a colt – Prince Charles knows how disappointed the Queen Mother becomes with the preponderance of fillies her mares produce which no steeple-chasing trainer really wants – which will become a good and compatible 'chaser for him to ride in the future.

Whatever other leisure pursuits beckon the Prince in the years to come, the majority will concern horses. As he says, he does genuinely love them. They bring him the pleasure and relaxation he deserves, and his rapport with those he rides is very apparent. And although a little brown pony now grazing at Sandringham was responsible, when she was a child, for breaking the Princess of Wales's arm and with it her nerve, she shares much of her husband's horse interest. She has also intimated she herself might start riding again one day, if 'very gently'.

Prince Charles looking relaxed and happy while practising polo in Deauville, France.

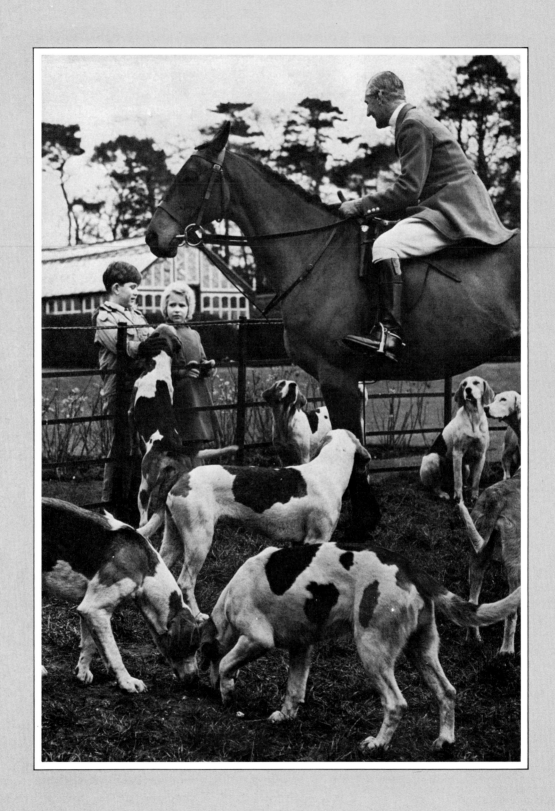

Chapter Ten

Princess Anne: Olympic Rider

PRINCESS ANNE has said that the chief reason she began riding as a child was because there were always horses and ponies 'around'. And certainly she had been brought up in a world where carriage horses, riding horses, polo ponies, police horses, and those of the Household Cavalry were, as they had been for most of the Queen's childhood, a part of the natural order, the clatter of hooves as familiar as the martial music that concludes the Changing of the Guard. Dan Maskell, who coached the Princess in tennis when she was 12 or so, also maintains that had she concentrated on the game she could have become a top-class player – like her grandfather King George VI, who played for the air force in a doubles match at Wimbledon when he was a young man. But whether due to that plethora of equines or not, Anne did not take up tennis seriously. From a young age she appeared to be as hooked on riding as any other 'pony-mad' child. As a toddler her favourite toys were an old rocking-horse belonging to the Queen, and one of Charles's ex-favourites, a wooden horse and cart that could be pedalled along. From almost the first time she sat on a pony she showed herself to be one of the lucky ones – something of a 'natural' and spared the imaginative terrors of a horse 'taking off' with her that beset Charles.

It was not long after the start of the era with the pony called William that Anne, keen and confident, progressed to going out on a leading rein beside the groom's horse. Within a short while and without any of the trouble the Queen experienced as a child in persuading the groom in charge to let her off the lead long after it was a necessary adjunct, Anne was happily coping with William 'on her own'. The Queen, a believer in doing things for oneself, taught Charles and Anne how to catch, and saddle and bridle their own ponies, and ensured they did not look on them as mere assets, to be produced ready to ride when required and removed by a groom afterwards. It was an involvement that came naturally to Anne and during the years she and Charles had intermittent riding lessons from Sybil Smith, the Princess took every chance to learn more about 'looking after a pony'. Since her marriage the opportunity of ordering and taking part in the lives of her own horses has added greatly to the enjoyment she gets from them. And Princess Anne's matter-of-course way of helping out with everything around the stables, from bandaging legs to mucking

January 1957. Prince Charles and Princess Anne at the West Norfolk Hunt's meet at Harpley. With them is Major R. Hoare, the Acting Master and Huntsman.

out, accounts partly for the regard and admiration she receives from her girl grooms.

William, and Greensleeves that both children rode, were succeeded by a good all-purpose pony called Mayflower, and then Bandit arrived on the scene. Anne had a great deal of fun with this pony. He furthered her liking for jumping and she achieved a good deal of success with him. Bandit also put a spark to her competitive spirit, although at the time competing formed only a very small part of her riding life. When the royal family went on holiday to Scotland or Norfolk Bandit went along too for riding around the estates, at Balmoral sometimes taking turns with one of the Fells. In those years Anne was being educated at home with a governess, and for the rest of the year she was able to ride at Windsor at weekends, as well as during the Easter holidays.

One joy of riding in the Home Park was the miniature cross-country course built for her by the Crown Equerry, and she and Bandit batted happily round the small fences, occasionally in the company of a few other young riders imported to share the fun. In the Easter Holidays the Crown Equerry sometimes organised a miniature hunter trial or other jumping competition, events much enjoyed by all, but to the Queen's embarrassment more often than not won by her daughter. It was not a question of having a better pony or riding a familiar course. Many of the other competitors were riding the equals of Bandit, and the fences were always newly constructed and untried. Anne often won because she was already showing the determination and will to win she inherits from her father, a trait which was to stand her in good stead in the future.

With the departure of the out-grown Bandit, Charles's interest in riding waned. The 14.2 Irish-bred High Jinks was brought in exclusively for Anne to ride. The pony had a good temperament and all-round potential but at four years old he had even less experience of competing than his new rider.

The Queen and Prince Philip might well have bought their daughter a brilliant 'made' pony that could have acted as schoolmaster, and was capable of whizzing its rider into the top levels of whatever form of junior competing she wished. But the royal family have always believed whenever possible in building up their own successes from scratch. As a child it suited Anne to have a challenge, and since Jinks was good material it was up to her to turn him to good use. In the years since she has been competing at the top of the eventing world the Princess has always brought on her own young horses, buying the right sort of animal, but never the ready 'made' one.

There was no great rush to start competing, in any form, and Jinks and his rider pottered along together, allowing a sensible time to get to know each other. There were now some show-jumps close by the castle golf course and 36 small fences on the Home Park cross-country. Apart from a dislike of ditches and water, a nonsense for an Irish-bred pony that was quickly overcome, Jinks obviously enjoyed jumping as much as Anne. She began taking him to the occasional Pony Club rally

The young Princess Anne at the Windsor Horse Show in May 1961.

and then to a few little competitions, mostly hunter trials and usually in a pairs class, where she and her partner scored one or two wins.

In the autumn of 1963, when she was 13, life changed considerably for both the Princess and her pony. At her own wish she went to boarding school, to Benenden School for Girls in Kent. After the initial term Jinks went along too, at livery in term-time at a first-class riding school conveniently close by. Anne was to ride him there once a week, instructed in a class of eight, by a horse trials devotee who had herself been a top-class event rider.

The Princess arrived in the class as an enthusiastic rider with good balance, sensitive hands, an old-fashioned 'seat', and the courage and ambition to get up on any horse or pony in sight. Her old-fashioned length of rein and stirrup leather also had to be amended, her tendency to the backward seat in jumping changed to a more modern position. A first acquaintance with dressage did not impress her. She thought it senseless and boring and, given the choice, would have confined her tuition to jumping fences at speed. Fortunately her instructor made no concessions and although a proportion of the lessons concerned show and cross-country riding and jumping, much of the time was spent in the covered school concentrating on the ground work that prepares horses and riders for everything else. When Anne found these proceedings too slow, she livened them up by pinching Jinks behind the saddle to make him buck.

By the following year the Princess's views had changed considerably and she and her pony were learning fast. At an open day at the riding school, when all competitors in one class had to ride school horses, she rode as a member of the Benenden 'A' team to win the Combined Training Cup – a competition consisting of a dressage test and show-jumping. To emphasise her change in outlook, she and Jinks then took second place in the individual Junior (14 years and under) Combined Training Cup, and a third in the dressage-only competition for the same age group. In the Easter holidays she took Jinks to a few minor Pony Club horse trials, where she enjoyed sufficient success to fan her ambitions.

Anne was also extending her experience of riding different horses and ponies, both at the riding school and at home in the mews at Windsor with any animal she was allowed to lay hands on. In those years she was frequently in and out of the mews but the horses were not the only reason – the stables were a good place to evade the holiday governess who was supposed always to be keeping an eye on her charge.

Princess Anne left school at the end of July 1968, just before her eighteenth birthday. On the public duty side of her life, as yet unstarted, the future was not very clear. In her private life she was feeling a little out of things. Her school-friends were all busy with jobs and flats of their own and all the things she could not do, and there had not yet been time for her to establish herself as an adult within the limits of royal restrictions. Like Prince Charles she wanted to prove to the world at large, and most of all to herself, what she could do, irrespective of who she was. In her case it seemed that horses could provide the means. If she could ride well and make a success of it, then it would be because she could ride . . . not because she was a Princess.

Anne was already sufficiently bitten with the excitement and problems of eventing, the most complete and testing of all equine competitions, to decide that it should be her chosen sport – although, she has said, given the chance it might well have been polo!

By the first months of 1968 she was making plans to achieve the difficult follow-through from junior eventing to the very different, much tougher world of adult horse trials. Alison Oliver, wife of the well-known former show-jumper, accepted a request to help and, since Jinks had already been relegated to the role of 'pleasure' pony, the first requirement was to find a suitable horse.

As so many young riders have discovered, the change-over from pony to horse is not purely a matter of size – in many, mostly indefinable ways the two have different characteristics and require a different approach. Here Anne was lucky in being used to riding horses in the mews, although the competing had been done with Jinks. She had, however, ridden Blue Star, a horse belonging to Sir John Miller, in a couple of hunter trials, and the animal was sent to Alison Oliver as a possible eventer for the Princess. For various reasons this did not work out, but the younger Purple Star, third in the line of seven 'Stars' all bred from Sir John's Stella, a former Olympic event horse, was chosen instead.

As a six-year-old Purple Star was untried except for two or three day's hunting and Alison rode him in a couple of novice events during Anne's last Easter term at school. The verdict was that this 15.3-hand bay gelding could be 'just right' for that stage of the Princess's riding, with both horse and rider starting their eventing career from scratch.

Anne made a first acquaintance with the Oliver's yard, the friendly, unpretentious surroundings that quickly became as familiar as the Windsor Mews, at the beginning of those Easter holidays. She came as often as possible, and arrived as one who was very happy and confident on horseback, but without any technical knowledge or previous opportunities to work horses from the training point of view and apply it to her own riding. Her only experience of eventing was with a pony, at Pony Club level, yet eight years later she was to be chosen as a member of the 1976 British Olympics eventing team. The gap between the two stages was so enormous that not even a whisper of such a goal could have entered Anne's most ambitious dream, and it was something that could never have been achieved without the utmost in concentrated hard work and co-operation from both pupil and instructor.

LEFT: *Princess Anne on Purple Star during the Showjumping Section of the Windsor Horse Trials in April 1968.*

RIGHT: *Royal Spectators: Prince Philip and Prince Andrew watching Princess Anne competing in the Dressage Section.*

Before the start Alison Oliver had wondered how it might go and was often to thank her lucky stars that Princess Anne is the person she is. If she had possessed less ability or had been difficult to work with it could have been a formidable job. As it was, the teaching, based on mutual enjoyment and interest, could not have been easier or the relationship more friendly, whether it was during a couple of hours' strenuous schooling in the paddock, or on a long drive with the horses to some distant competition. The key-note was the shared determination to get things right and progress. The Princess has the same capacity as the Queen quickly to appreciate and act on what is being put over, and the same rapport with the horses she rides.

In the circumstances it might have been expected that Anne would arrive far better equipped than any of the Olivers' other clients. In fact her 'tack' was quite inadequate and had gradually to be replaced, and the entire form of her previous riding needed to be moulded into a totally different kind of set-up. She had good balance, a good seat which had only to be slightly changed, and a great deal of natural 'feel' and rhythm. Otherwise there was much to learn.

The right outlook is one of the essentials to successful competing and here Anne is lucky with her inheritance of Prince Philip's determination and ability to rise to the occasion. Never ruthless, willing to give a horse an 'easy' if that accords with the training plan, the Princess otherwise enters every event all out to win if she can but never, like some, just to have a 'jolly ride'. Like everyone else she gets 'strung up' beforehand but is not in the least nervous. In the very early days she occasionally showed her annoyance when things went wrong – as Prince Charles knows so well it does not help at these times to be the focal point of public attention – but the attitude of the other riders at the Olivers' yard was a great help. These were people who were only too often having to accept that a horse can be brilliant at one competition and have an 'off day' at the next. It was an atmosphere that Anne soon absorbed and it helped her to the right assessment of life with horses – to shrug off the disappointments as 'just one of those things' or, tongue in cheek, quoting one of Alison's favoured maxims: 'Well, it's all good experience . . .!'

As was hoped, Purple Star proved to be exactly right for the transition from pony to horse. Nowadays Prince Edward is appreciating the little horse's marked personality, still very quick both in thinking and reactions and occasionally far too clever. Anne found him enjoyably fast across country, with a lot of jumping ability and capable of very good dressage – when he could be bothered to pay attention. In those days of his youth he could also be very naughty, particularly on arrival at an event. To seize a momentary lapse in concentration by his rider and scamper across to the other side of a dressage arena, was Purple's idea of an equine joke. It was a sense of humour he sometimes brought to his jumping. Never very fond of jumping into water, when Anne once gave him a strong aid at the Windsor lake jump, Purple retaliated by making an enormous leap out into the deep water and taking her for a swim.

The Queen and Princess Anne watching competitors during the Eridge Horse Trials in August 1968. Alison Oliver is standing on the left.

This was just the sort of character to appeal to the Princess and he provided the challenge she enjoys. Alison schooled rider and horse throughout those Easter holidays, their good progress marked by winning the Senior Individual at the South Oxfordshire Pony Club Horse Trials. They then wound up with a most satisfactory eighth overall at Windsor, in Anne's first adult one-day event.

Before leaving school she had a change of venue and type of competition by riding a loaned horse as one of four riders in fancy dress, in a team competing for the Eldonian Quadrille Championships at the 1968 Horse of the Year Show. Apart from this diversion, all through that autumn Anne and Purple were competing in as many novice horse trials as possible, and having the satisfaction of being consistently placed.

Since those days Princess Anne has ridden and competed with many horses of many different types and there are few she has not regarded with affection. Purple Star was one of the 'specials', the horse that set her on the road to success and provided her with a lot of fun on the way. As she says: 'He was never a particularly easy passage,' but for that era he 'had all that was required.' It was only in the later days he began stopping when he thought he had got himself seriously 'wrong' at a fence, and he did have the quickest 'stop' Anne has ever encountered. She not infrequently found herself continuing on her way over his head. Eventually Purple made it plain that his eventing days were over and he retired to the enjoyments of the hunting field before, fit and well but in his twenties, providing Prince Edward with a lot of pleasure.

By the spring of 1969 Anne was competing with both Purple and Royal Ocean, a big long-striding Thoroughbred from Ireland, with the speed developed on the race-track. He was a reliable horse but lacking Purple's 'spark' and personality, qualities that also seemed to characterise a young horse newly arrived from Sandringham that Alison was assessing.

This was Doublet, a six-year old chestnut by Doubtless II, an Argentinian racehorse that raced in England, out of Suerte, once one of Prince Philip's favourite polo ponies. At nearly 16.2 Doublet had grown too big for polo so was sent along as a possible event horse for the Princess. He had been difficult as a youngster but although still very sensitive and needing understanding, there was something about the horse that convinced Alison he was out of the ordinary. Anne was not so sure.

All through April she had been gaining a lot of experience, and usually at least a place, in various novice horse trials, with one satisfactory fourth with Purple in a foxhunter show-jumping class. At times her fortunes were mixed. At one event Royal Ocean was ridden with such determination at a 'drop' fence where Purple had stopped in a previous round, the big horse met it wrong and fell. On another day Anne collected a first and a second with the two of them in a novice Combined Training competition. Before the end of the month Purple Star had been upgraded and Anne entered him in the intermediate section, and Royal Ocean in the novice, at the Windsor Horse Trials. On the day Purple was coughing and a non-starter, but with Ocean the Princess, one of 27 starters for that section, had a convincing win – eight points ahead of a young soldier called Mark Phillips.

By then Alison was certain of Doublet's ability and potential, and that he was the perfect kind of horse for Anne to take on, demanding that much more of her as a rider than her other horses but ultimately with much more to give. Anne was still not sure and the original schooling sessions with Doublet were not a great success. She felt she did not combine with the horse and at one stage considered it unlikely she ever would. However, with faith in her trainer's judgement she thought the fault must lie with herself and accepted this new challenge with her usual resolution.

By this time Princess Anne's public life was coming to the fore and her riding had to be fitted in accordingly. Except for that first autumn of 1968, like other members of her family she has never been able to give anything approaching the time to training most competitors consider essential. As Charles found with his race training, often the only way was to get up at the crack of dawn and drive to the Olivers' for a schooling session, before going on to some public engagement. Alison kept the horses fit and in work for her when it was impossible to do so herself, but there was no question of the animals being schooled and produced ready for her just to ride 'on the day'. Nothing could be further removed from the Princess's outlook and anyway, as every horseman knows, it would not have worked, but such was the irritating suggestion occasionally put forward by the ignorant when Anne first started to prove that she was a competitor to be reckoned with.

The Princess has always known that the only path to real success in the horse world is to realise Prince Charles's ambition of forming an ideal partnership with one's horse. As the weeks went by and her understanding with Doublet increased, this relationship for which Alison had hoped, gradually became established. In public together for the first time on June 26 1969, Anne rode Doublet to win a dressage competition at Basingstoke. A month later a win in the novice class of the chestnut's first horse trials, qualified him, like Royal Ocean, for the Midland Bank Novice Event Championships at Chatsworth on October 18.

Before that date there were satisfactory placings in various one-day events – three seconds and a third, with an eighth and eleventh position as the lowest. At the Chatsworth championships Anne and Doublet ended the season with a pleasing sixth over a tough course. The day was only marred by Royal Ocean's uncharacteristic three refusals during his round of the cross-country. Later the horse was found to be slightly unfit and he was retired to Windsor as a riding horse, eventually filling in part of the year as a police horse.

At every stage of her riding the Princess knew she had the Queen's full support and interest and when eventing came up it was a sport of which the Queen already had prior knowledge. The royal family have always enjoyed their annual private visit to the Badminton three-day horse trials and in 1956 only the worst of bad luck prevented the Queen's horse, Countryman, and his rider, Bertie Hill, from winning the individual Gold Medal for eventing at the Stockholm Olympics. And although when Anne started eventing Prince Philip thought it unlikely she would reach international level, he was proud of her initial successes and well understood the competitive spirit that matched his own. At the same time both he and the Queen felt it might be a good thing if their daughter could find another interest as well as horses.

In the days when Anne was competing with Jinks the Queen had occasionally been able to go along and watch without attracting undue publicity. But those times were as much in the past as the comfortingly small fences the Princess and her pony used to negotiate. Even the novice fences the Queen was now looking at in photographs seemed formidable by comparison, and it was nice to know there was someone of Alison Oliver's unruffled competence to help with Anne's increasingly ambitious riding programme.

In 1969 the Princess went on her first state visit, accompanying the Queen and Prince Philip to Austria. Whilst there she was given the opportunity to ride Siglavy Bona, a Lipizzaner stallion, amidst the baroque splendours of the famous Spanish Riding School. These horses and their riders require years of the most meticulous training to achieve the rigorous and specialised demands of haute école, and Anne was pleased when under the instruction of the late Colonel Johann Handler she managed a modest 'piaffe'. This is a lofty trot performed on one spot, which she thought '. . . very remarkable and satisfying . . . provided one can get it right!' She little thought that before many years, getting movements equivalent to a piaffe 'right' might be a requirement of the dressage tests she would have to assimilate for international eventing.

The Princess's widely publicised horse interests quite often provided her with the opportunity to ride some unfamiliar types of horses during a break from duty on official visits abroad. In Hong Kong there was a 'country bred' she rode to look across the border into China. She had an unexpectedly hilarious ride on an ex-racehorse in New Zealand, and in Australia made the acquaintance of a stock horse, that still indispensable adjunct to parts of the outback. When in Kenya the Princess, as President of the Save the Children Fund, was filmed riding for the BBC's Blue Peter programme, her mount a co-operative polo pony. On safari in Ethiopia it was a rather less co-operative mule.

In 1971 when Prince Philip and the Princess were in Iran representing the Queen at the late Shah's Coronation celebrations at Persepolis, she was taken to the royal stables at Farahabad, outside Tehran, to inspect the horses. The Shah was a fine horseman and a lover of speed and Anne was invited to ride the three-year-old Baldershine, one of his favourite stallions. The horse was one of a new breed then being evolved, part Thoroughbred/Persian Plateau X Jadran Arab, and although well mannered and schooled was as fiery as all Persian horses. Accompanied by the British Military Attaché and Mrs Firouz, who discovered the Caspian ponies, the Princess had the excitement of testing Baldershine's speed when they left the rough moufflon trails amongst the Elburz range, and headed back for Farahabad at the gallop on a five-mile sweep round from the mountains. Anne's horsemanship did not go unremarked that day. Before leaving the country she was presented with Awtash, meaning 'fire', a bay colt of that same 'Pahlavan' breed (named after the Shah's dynasty).

Quarantine regulations delayed the arrival of Awtash in England for some time, but he came eventually and was for a while worked at Robert Hall's well known Fulmer School of Equitation in Buckinghamshire. He was then loaned to a lady rider who has also used him to a certain extent for breeding.

In a very different context, another new involvement with horses began in 1972, and has continued as an ever growing and most worthwhile interest. This occurred when the Princess became Patron of the Riding for the Disabled Association. She had always thought riding for those with physical and mental disabilities might be a good idea but knew very little then of the marvellous therapy it has proved to be or the rapid growth of the movement.

Some 500 years before the birth of Christ the ancient Greeks were aware that riding a horse was good treatment for those suffering from incurable diseases, chiefly on the theory that suffering becomes easier to bear when there is something else of interest to occupy the mind. To some extent the idea persisted through the ages, and after World War I injured soldiers convalescing at Oxford Hospital were encouraged to ride as part of their therapeutic treatment. By the fifties and sixties small pioneer groups were fostering the thought that riding could be good for many kinds of disablement. They needed a public boost and it came when Liz Hartnell, a Dane with partially paralysed legs, became the first woman to win an Olympic medal for dressage.

The Advisory Council on Riding for the Disabled was formed in 1964 and succeeded five years later by the present association. At that time there were 80 groups up and down the country, catering for about 2000 disabled people. By the end of 1981 there were more than 500 groups looking after around 14,000 riders and, despite an inner city service developing plans and the building of other centres, without increasing facilities they are unable to provide for the enormous waiting list.

At first the medical profession was sceptical but the obvious hope and enjoyment it gave to thousands of children and adults made them change their view. It is all made possible with the loan of suitable ponies and through the time given by the bands of devoted volunteer helpers. But there are other important factors attached to this work and the Princess is glad that, although the movement never stops growing, it has not been allowed to grow too fast. Before starting a new group people have learned to stop and think about how much more there is to it than just having some ponies and the use of a school.

As Patron the Princess's name, and the interest and energy she

Princess Anne and Prince Charles enjoying a ride together.

expends in being so much more than a figurehead, are a tremendous help and booster to the RDA. She tries to get round all the groups in the country to see for herself some of the problems as well as the rewards. Over and over she has witnessed the ecstatic look of achievement of someone, condemned to life in a wheelchair, when they are moving around on the back of a led pony supported by helpers. She loves to see how often handicapped children and the ponies relate to each other, and to hear of the miracle when an autistic child who has never spoken says a word to his mount.

Princess Anne has many public commitments, many that are not reported by the national press, but the Save the Children Fund, of which she is President, and the Riding for the Disabled Association have always claimed the lion's share of her time and attention.

By the spring of 1970 Anne and Doublet were entered for their first three-day event at Tidworth but owing to a minor injury Purple Star, by then upgraded to Open, had to substitute for the chestnut. Alison Oliver was having a baby and the horses had been moved temporarily to Lars Sederholm's establishment. The Princess, who had been in Australia with the Queen and Prince Philip, went straight there on her

return to do a get-fit crash course before Tidworth, riding three horses that afternoon and two more the following morning before breakfast. She had an idea Lars was not very impressed with Purple, and it gave her a lot of satisfaction during a training gallop to be able to leave him and his horse standing.

Unfortunately at Tidworth things did not go so well. They were lying fifth at the end of the dressage, but then two refusals across country and one of Purple's lightning stops in the show-jumping, that sent his rider sailing on ahead, left them finishing well down the line. The next morning the papers were showing pictures of Anne's spectacular fall but that was only to be expected. What she did find aggravating was the quote of what she was supposed to have said. It was a comment she might well have made, but had been too surprised to say anything at all! After the event she and Lars took Purple Star back onto the cross-country and schooled him over the fences he had refused. Anne always felt her little horse never forgave her for that, and Tidworth virtually marked the end of his eventing career.

By 1971 the Princess had her sights on Badminton, the prestigious three-day event to which, unless precluded by school terms, she had accompanied her family since a child, looking with awe at the famous fences. Now her family would be watching her and Doublet tackling them. All through the previous year they had been getting as much experience as possible, competing in foxhunter show-jumping classes, dressage tests, and combined training competitions. They were well in the public eye, but as Anne frequently used just one or two of the phases of a horse trial as a school, it was difficult for the knowledgeable to assess her and Doublet's true potential.

There were many who doubted if the Princess would ever 'make' Badminton, either through lack of ability or because the Queen would consider it too dangerous. Those ignorant of how tough this sport the French descriptively call 'Concours Complet d'Equitation' really is, considered she would of course win. (Shades of that curious outlook Prince Charles was to encounter later. . . .) Apart from the shortened version at Tidworth, Badminton was to be the first three-day event for Anne and her horse – and experience counts for a lot in this sport. Excitement grew as the weeks slipped by towards April 22. Would the Princess get round? Had she the right horse? Was her riding as good as some made out?

In early April Anne took Doublet to Rushall, then the accepted 'school' for Badminton. In the Open International class she gained a pleasing 36 for dressage, one point ahead of Mark Phillips, that young soldier, still only an acquaintance, against whom she frequently competed. Mark won without adding to his penalty points, Anne went clear over the show-jumps, then collected 22 time faults with a deliberately unhurried but impressive cross-country, to finish fourth.

That year the Queen, Prince Philip, the Queen Mother and other members of the royal family arrived as usual to stay at Badminton

Princess Anne and Doublet taking one of the cross-country obstacles in the Crookham Horse Trials at Tweseldown Racecourse in March 1972.

House, their normal interest in the event considerably heightened. The foreign competitors, their horses quartered with all the others in the Duke of Beaufort's stabling, had come in from Holland, Switzerland, and Sweden. With the numbers of top-notch British and Irish riders, including the holders of the individual World and European Champion titles, they presented a formidable opposition.

After the first day's dressage the Princess and Doublet were in the lead and remained there until late afternoon on the second day when Mark Phillips and his horse, Great Ovation, took over by 7 points.

The next day, Saturday, when the speed and endurance section always takes place, the rain was bucketing down, producing very tricky conditions for the competitors, a sea of mud for the thousands of spectators, and a dreadful aftermath in his lovely park for the Duke of Beaufort to contemplate when it was all over. Anne went off number 20 out of the 48 starters. By then the rain had stopped, the wind had dried out the ground a little, but she was not expecting to get round. She did not

think her trainer expected her to get round either, but this was refuted by Alison Oliver. If the Princess and Doublet had not been ready they would not have been at Badminton. Given a modicum of the necessary luck, Alison felt the combination would do better than most, but the going could be the unpredictable factor.

They collected 32 time penalties on the steeplechase. On the cross-country there were one or two well sat 'pecks' on the soggy landings and 42.4 time penalties, but none for jumping. Beyond all expectations the Princess and Doublet ended the day in fourth place. Mark Phillips, still with only his dressage penalties, was well in the lead, almost 20 points ahead of Mary Gordon-Watson, with Richard Walker lying third.

At Badminton the show-jumping phase takes place on Sunday afternoon, after the veterinary inspection of the morning. As usual the competitors jumped in reverse order of merit. The Princess came in fourth from last, with no chance of winning but knowing it needed only one error to push them down a place. They had their error, at the unfamiliar water jump, which Anne says filled Doublet with amazement. Whatever the reason he had a foot in it and they dropped one place. But a fifth at a first attempt at Badminton – that and Burghley being the most important three-day events in the world – was a wonderful achievement, reflecting great credit on rider, horse, and trainer, and a source of great pride and satisfaction for the royal family.

Mark Phillips won and for the first of four occasions had the honour of receiving his trophy from the Queen.

The next ambition was the European Championships at Burghley in the autumn. There was growing excitement about whether Princess Anne would be asked to be a member of the team representing Great Britain. There was no question of the polished performance at Badminton being a fluke, both rider and horse had demonstrated their quality in all three phases, but they still lacked experience and it was an international competition. The Princess was not included in the short-list from which the team would be chosen, but she was invited, if all went well, to compete as one of the 12 individual riders Britain, as host country, was allowed to enter.

Princess Anne's laconic description of the run-up to Burghley is that she was in Canada in May and in hospital by the middle of July. There was rather more to it than that. A major operation six weeks before the selectors' final trial at Eridge, in a sport that demands the ultimate in fitness of both rider and horse, seemed bound to put paid to Anne's aspirations for that season. But even Alison Oliver seemed to forget that like 'protocol', 'impossible' is not a word to which Anne takes kindly. When Alison went to the hospital to commiserate she found the patient busy working out a crash course for getting fit.

It still seemed an impossibility, but a combination of 'guts', determination, and youth was to win the day. The Princess came out of hospital and was then given a book of exercises by a physiotherapist which, against her natural inclinations, she performed faithfully. She

Princess Anne out riding on Purple Star in 1969.

spent a week at Balmoral walking up and down hills, then a week on the royal yacht, *Britannia*, taking as much exercise as she could. She got back four days before Eridge and started riding. It seemed all right and Alison had kept Doublet fit.

They were leading after the dressage phase at Eridge. The cross-country had its moment when Doublet jumped too far up a bank coming out of the water to negotiate the rail on landing. He stopped and Anne fell off. It did not matter. It was something that could have happened to anyone and the selectors disregarded it. Anne herself was thrilled. She was feeling none the worse and Doublet had gone so well. Despite the slip-up they had the equal fastest time of the day across country. Burghley was on.

The crowds were enormous but Doublet, a great showman, rose to the occasion, despite the pressures, concentrating to produce a lovely rhythmic and accurate test. When the dressage marks went up there were only 41.5 penalty points and the Princess was in first place, 7.5 marks better than Mühin of the USSR. This surprised those of the overseas contingent who had heard of Princess Anne and her horse but never seen them in action. They felt an eventing Princess added prestige to the sport but could scarcely be counted as a serious rival. Even those good dressage marks would be of little use if the remaining phases were not comparable, and there was a long way to go yet – at a rough estimate about 18 miles and 43 fences.

With no penalties on the steeplechase, and with the double section of roads and tracks, the veterinary inspection, and the 10-minute breather behind them, the Princess set off on the 4-mile, 1324-yard gallop interspersed with 33 fair but searching fences. She need not have worried that Doublet might not like the hard going, and apart from a slip coming out of the Trout Hatchery when he nearly fell, there were no problems. Implementing decisions already taken on how to tackle any tricky fences, Anne rode Doublet at them with sufficient determination to give him the confidence to take off, meet them just right, and gallop on in the cadence of his ground-covering stride. They went clear in the second fastest time. Before the show-jumping they were holding a lead of 27.8 points, and they jumped a clear round.

It was a great day for Britain. The British won the team event, in which Mark was riding to come sixth over all, and Princess Anne became Individual European Eventing Champion. It was a wonderful day for the Queen, presenting the Raleigh Trophy to her daughter who had ridden a home-bred horse to victory and for Prince Philip, full of pride and delighted to have been proved wrong about Anne's original ambitions being a little too high.

Altogether 1971 was a superlative year for the Princess. She won the Sportswriters' Award, was named the Daily Express Sportswoman of the Year, and the BBC Television Sports Personality of the Year. But as Anne knows, and as everyone connected with horses has to learn, the luck comes, and the luck goes.

Princess Anne competing on Doublet in the Calia Insurance Mid-Summer Dressage Championship at Barham Park, Wembley, in July 1973.

After Burghley Doublet developed leg trouble, possibly caused by treading on himself in that slip at the Trout Hatchery. It was not thought to be serious, but after a very thorough work-out during the last preparations for the 1972 Badminton, it had to be accepted that the strained tendon might not stand up to it, and he was 'roughed off' for a year. There was a moment, wisely discarded, when it was thought that Anne might possibly ride Columbus at Badminton. But that year the Princess went to the three-day event as a spectator and saw Mark Phillips and Great Ovation win for the second year running. There was then no idea that seven months after the next Badminton they would be married.

Chapter Eleven

Anne and Mark: Eventing Successes

A ROUND A couple of months before Princess Anne was born Mark Phillips won his first rosette. It was in a leading-rein class, he was riding a hairy little Shetland led by his mother, and he was not quite two years old.

Horses were an integral part of the Phillips family. Mark's parents rode and hunted, his father considered competing the best thing possible to interest a boy in riding well, and his mother ensured that ponies and riding were fun. His aunt, Miss Flavia Phillips who lives in the same village as his parents, was to help and encourage Mark in every way.

In such an atmosphere riding came in the natural order of things and when, aged four, he fell off his second pony and broke his arm, unlike many small boys it had little effect on Mark's confidence or, once mended, on his enjoyment. By the age of six he was riding Pickles, a 13.2-hand pony. At seven, Mark and Pickles were hunting regularly and jumping quite sizable fences. They also went to gymkhanas, hunter trials, shows, and the Pony Club competitions put on by the local branch which Mark had joined when he was five. When he was eight he and Pickles won a working pony class at Badminton, where similar classes used to be held in conjunction with the three-day event. It was the first of three wins in successive years and each time he had the excitement of receiving his prize from the Queen.

When Mark was nine his family moved to their present home at Great Somerford in Wiltshire. He then joined the Beaufort Branch of the Pony Club, and that brought him the good fortune of being trained by two ex-Olympic eventing riders. In the early years he was schooled by Colonel Alec Scott who taught him a great deal about dressage and show-jumping, and later by Colonel Frank Weldon, winner of a team gold and the individual bronze at Stockholm in 1956, whose particular field has always been the cross-country.

From the first, Mark's riding attracted attention and at the unusually early age of twelve he and Archer, a newly acquired 14.2-hand pony, were chosen for the Beaufort team being trained by Colonel Scott for the 1960 Pony Club Eventing Championships. Mark has said it is the story of his life to return to earth with a bump just when things have been going well, and after an excellent dressage score Archer, probably the

Princess Anne on Goodwill and Captain Mark Phillips on Columbus at the Badminton Horse Trials.

best schooled pony he ever owned, was eliminated for three refusals at the water on the cross-country course. Fortunately, Mark's instructors, who by then included Molly Sivewright of the Talland School of Equitation, were unshaken in their faith in his abilities. He was included in the Beaufort team for the next four years, reaching the finals on three occasions. As he was educated at boarding school riding was always confined to the holidays, but while at Marlborough Mark suffered a back injury that precluded rugger and brought riding even more to the fore. By that time he was being instructed by Colonel Weldon who considered him 'one of the best riders in the Pony Club'.

By chance, the ponies and later the horses of Mark's youth were all very different, which gave him the valuable experience of coping with widely dissimilar animals. In that first Pony Club final he was partnered by Pirate, a bold jumper that was so sensitive his rider had to develop equally sensitive hands. After that it was Kookaburra, Kookie to his family, a quality cob owned by Mark's aunt, that had the ability to go along with him into the first stages of adult eventing, but always needed pushing.

In the first season of adult novice one-day events Mark and Kookie had one win and were consistently placed, but this standard was the limit of the cob's capabilities. The search was then on for a horse that could cope with Mark's rapidly growing ambitions.

Captain Mark Phillips and Lincoln after winning the Badminton Horse Trials for the fourth time in April 1981.

The six-year-old 16.1-hand gelding, Rock On, was, according to Mark, a 'mad devil' when bought and remained both headstrong and impetuous. He was an amazing jumper in more senses than one, sometimes dealing, quite successfully, with the largest fence by going straight up and down all four legs together like a flying bedstead. He was also so bold he would tackle anything without hesitation, including such impossibilities as a brook followed by two large steps cut into a bank, constituting two jumps that Rock On endeavoured, unsuccessfully, to fly as though they were one.

Mark left school in 1966 with two aims in view: to follow the family tradition by going into the army and to concentrate all his spare time on horse trials. There were four months at his disposal before joining up as a rifleman in the Green jackets, the first step towards being selected for officer training at Sandhurst and eventually to a commission in his father's old regiment, the Queen's Dragoon Guards. He decided to spend time with Rock On training in Devon with Bertie Hill, the official trainer of the British Olympic eventing team. Bertie Hill remembers him as 'one of the easiest and best pupils' he ever had, 'a natural rider'. Bertie also formed a high opinion of Rock On, admiring the horse's scope and courage, certain that the only problem was one of brakes – a trouble he was able to help alleviate if not entirely cure.

Mark and Rock On competed in their first three-day event at Burghley in 1967 where they finished a pleasing fourth. They repeated the placing at Badminton in 1968 and were then short-listed for the Olympic Games in Mexico that year, but sadly the horse was never to realise his true potential. His preparation for important events had often been interrupted by slight injuries and on the day before the final trial for the Olympics he broke down. It was a great disappointment, but Mark was paid the high compliment of being chosen as reserve rider to the British team, which consisted of Major Allhusen on Lochinvar, Jane Bullen on Our Nobby, Richard Meade on Cornishman V, and Ben Jones on The Poacher. Although he was not required as a replacement, which could also have meant standing in for a dressage or show-jumping rider, Mark enjoyed himself enormously – he learned a lot from the way the winning British team tackled the cross-country under those notorious conditions of torrential rain and mud.

After Mexico, Mark's sights were on the European Championships being held in France the following year. Rock On was not ready for Badminton in 1969, but the selectors of the team for France asked his rider to prove the horse's fitness in August, at the Punchestown three-day event in Ireland. After the dressage they were lying third but with a technical refusal on the cross-country dropped back to tenth. Much more serious was the fact that the luckless Rock On had staked himself and did not contest the final day. He recovered in time for Mark to be included as an individual for the event at Haras du Pin, where the fences were so enormous his rider lost concentration at what appeared to be the only innocuous one on the course, and they turned turtle. That cost him third place in the line-up to finish seventh. Despite the fall and one refusal he and Rock On still had the fastest time across country, over a course that was only completed by 22 of the starters, and only produced seven clear rounds.

Shortly after Haras du Pin, Rock On went lame again and was not fit to compete for two years, when Mark rode him to take fifth place in the 'Mini-Munich'. Sadly he died in 1972 after a tendon operation, which had nothing to do with his sudden collapse, and a post mortem revealed that it was due to a detached nodule in the aorta. It was something that could have occurred at any time.

In 1970 Mark was given the ride in the British World Championship team on Bertie Hill's Chicago III, because as a professional the horse's owner/rider did not qualify. Unfortunately, that course at Punchestown has gone down in eventing history as a 'shambles'. The fences were not as big as at Haras du Pin but were trappy and so narrow all the competitors had to jump in the same place. As it was pouring with rain the approaches and landings became terribly slippery, and were made worse by spectators walking the course, who without any provision for going round fences, climbed over the top. Mary Gordon-Watson and Cornishman V put up the best performance of their distinguished career by being one of the four clear rounds, and in the fastest time, but only 21 out of 40 starters completed the course, with only two countries, Britain and France, in at the finish. Nineteen horses were out before reaching what became the bogie – fence number 29 – and eight of those who did finish had a fall at this fence.

Up to this point Chicago had been going brilliantly, but fell trying to bank the wide parallel filled with deceptively solid-looking branches of fir, with a big drop on the far side. As Mark was picking himself up a 'helpful' spectator led the horse out beside the fence, instead of straight on under the far rail and so through the requisite flags. This meant they had to go back and jump the obstacle again, which they achieved with no trouble, but the spectators were crowding in so close that Chicago slipped and fell again as he turned sharply to avoid them.

Despite the tribulations they finished in eleventh place, a clear in the show-jumping also clinching the team prize for Britain, and with Mark's admiration for Bertie Hill's horse considerably enhanced. He was hoping to continue the partnership, which could have led to Olympic hopes, but before the next season's Badminton Chicago had been sold to Germany.

Mark rode Great Ovation at the 1971 Badminton principally to give himself 'the ride'. He owned the horse in partnership with his aunt, but despite a previous victory in the intermediate section of the Rushall Horse Trials, followed by a third in the advanced class at Liphook, no-one connected with Great Ovation thought he had much chance of getting round at Badminton, let alone being placed. Mark had ridden him in a few one-day trials in 1970, but 'Cheers' (his nickname) had a dangerous propensity to 'miss out' on the occasional fence, resulting in several falls, and did nothing to give his rider much confidence in the animal's future as an eventer. He fell again when being given a taste of international events at Deurne in Holland, and by the end of that season Mark and his aunt had almost decided to sell the horse. However, during the winter when Mark's regiment was stationed at Catterick, he was able to hunt Great Ovation with the Bedale and the Zetland, and as a result the horse began showing a little more promise when competing in hunter trials in the following spring. It was agreed to give him another chance.

Mark and Great Ovation won Badminton that year and, although the horse appeared to need more pushing across country, they won again in the succeeding year of 1972, where Princess Anne was watching from the side-lines. That victory gained Mark and his horse a place on the short-list for the Olympics, held at Munich in the autumn. At the final selection trial at Eridge a day's rain transformed good going into a treacherous morass and made the stream at fence 23 almost unnegotiable. Several Olympic hopes fell there, including Great Ovation, but it made no difference to being included in the team. Where it did make a difference, in Mark's estimation, was in his horse's approach to jumping across country. He had hated the slippery going and a fall at the water was the last straw.

During the week of preparation in Munich Mark had a feeling his horse was not 'quite right', but there was nothing he could 'put his finger on'. Great Ovation produced the best dressage of the British team and was to jump clear in the show-jumping. Over the cross-country course he had two falls and two refusals. It was 'one of those things' in life with horses and with Mark's score discarded, Richard Meade and Laurieston went on brilliantly to retrieve the British fortunes – a gold for the team, and the individual gold for himself.

Princess Anne was in Munich to watch that thrilling result before returning home to continue her training with Columbus for Burghley, later in the month. She had ridden him in their first three-day event together at Tidworth earlier in the year, where turning a circle in order to reduce speed, followed by further braking and steering problems that resulted in refusals at two fences, ensured their finishing well down the line. Anne says Columbus never took off with her when approaching a fence and never looked like giving her a fall, but on a long gallop between fences he pulled like a train and could become unstoppable. Before Burghley she and Alison seemed to have found the solution to the cross-country, a gag-snaffle that could be applied if necessary, but for some reason it was omitted for the steeplechase phase. Columbus began gathering speed to the extent where it seemed only sensible, if and when the Princess could stop, to pull out – but afterwards Anne admits to being annoyed with herself for the decision. Later she had to admit that the Queen's big strong horse needed a man to control him, and although she did not know Mark Phillips very well she thought he would be the most suitable. She had seen enough of his riding to know he was very strong, but also very sympathetic to different types of horse. With the Queen's

LEFT: *Immaculately turned out Captain Mark Phillips reassuring his horse before a competition.*

RIGHT: *Mid-flight. Princess Anne on Columbus taking an obstacle on the cross-country course at the Windsor Horse Trials in April 1972.*

approval Mark began, in that autumn of 1972, to try to come to terms with the impetuous, talented Columbus.

Since both Columbus and Doublet were the Queen's horses and kept with Alison Oliver, there was nothing particularly significant about the Princess and Mark training there together for Badminton in the early weeks of 1973. The press thought otherwise and, convinced of a romance, began haunting the Olivers' establishment until the necessary concentration at most of the training sessions became almost impossible. At the time, although Princess Anne and Captain Mark Phillips were to marry in November that year, it was the horses that were still the main preoccupation and the excessive attentions of the press were not welcomed. After Badminton there was a private engagement, but it was understandable that in an effort to have a little peace the news was kept within the family before being publicly announced some six weeks later. In the meantime the press stepped up their vigilance. When Mark brought out Columbus and Great Ovation at Cirencester, where Princess Anne rode his good horse Persian Holiday as well as her own Flame Gun, more than a hundred press photographers flocked to the event, coming from France, Italy, and Germany as an addition to the British contingent.

During the spring luck was not with Mark. A horse came down with him at Amberley and the following week Columbus fell at Rushall, for the second time that season, and his rider suffered concussion and the temporary loss of sight in one eye.

Things were going better for the Princess. Doublet's leg trouble, the legacy from their triumph at Burghley, was on the mend, and she was schooling Goodwill, a 16.2-hand eight-year-old that the Queen had bought the previous autumn on the advice of Alison Oliver. The horse had been hunted in his youth and then show-jumped, where he reached Grade A exceptionally quickly but then did not quite come up to expectations. He seemed to associate show-jumps with undue pressure, as Anne discovered the first time she tried him and was carted straight over four jumps without having a say in the matter. She found him quite different – happy and relaxed – on the novice cross-country at Smiths Lawn, where he was jumping the type of fences not seen since his hunting days. Goodwill has always possessed boundless energy but at first he did not seem to know how to control it. He appeared too strong for himself and when asked to gallop he did not know how, his legs 'all over the place', his nose near the ground – a tendency he was not to lose for some while and one that is very tiring for a rider trying to haul his head up at the approach to each fence.

By the time Badminton was in sight Goodwill was a much improved horse. Unlike Doublet, a showman at heart with the initial advantage of a natural cadence and presence, dressage was never to be the brown horse's strong point. He improved with experience but never lost the capacity to give a good impression of a volcano about to erupt. It was Goodwill's limitless scope and courage, the ability to throw an enormous leap if meeting a spread a long way off, that made him the great horse he was to become.

Captain Mark Phillips on Great Ovation competing at the Amberley Horse Show, Cirencester, in March 1973.

In 1973 it had been decided to try out a new dressage test at Badminton, one that was strongly criticised by the competitors as quite unsuited to bold cross-country horses, and was subsequently dropped. The test included flying-changes, a standard of dressage for which Goodwill was not prepared. He boiled up and got himself into a 'state', with the inevitable consequence of low marks, but apart from a technical refusal, then performed a very commendable cross-country and pulled up to a satisfactory eighth place in the whole event.

Goodwill was not the only one to come under pressure at that Badminton. It was Mark's chance to achieve a record by winning the classic event for the third successive year with the same horse. But his jinx was still around and Great Ovation was withdrawn lame after the 'roads and tracks'. He had the ride on Columbus to come and it was still possible to make it a third win in a row for himself, but after some of their tribulations together he did not feel very sanguine and his feelings proved prophetic. Columbus fell twice on the cross-country – a spectacular crash at one of the Luckington Lane fences, over rails at the edge of a bank with a fearsome drop, and then again with a nose-dive into the lake.

After that performance many were to tell Mark he was a fool to ride such a dangerous horse, but he only grinned and bet Mike Tucker five pounds he and Columbus would finish in the first three at Badminton the next year. His faith in the horse was unshaken and he knew that somewhere there was a key to their problems.

It lay with that gag-snaffle which Anne had used as a confidence-giving hand-brake, ready for emergencies but never operated coming into a fence. Columbus was used to making his own arrangements about the actual jumping and therefore when Mark, a strong rider who normally 'places' his horse at a fence, employed the gag, the horse began thinking back to his rider instead of concentrating on where he was going. Mark had the strength to hold Columbus on the flat in an ordinary snaffle with a figure-of-eight noseband, and when the gag was removed their difficulties went with it.

That autumn the Princess was to have the chance of defending her European title at the championships to be held at Kiev. Hopefully Doublet was completely recovered and would obviously partner her, but if there was an unimaginable snag Anne, unlike some people, was confident Goodwill was capable of the job. Even so, when she took Doublet, showing every sign of being his old self, to the final trial at Osberton, Goodwill was very much the understudy. He had to take over the star role in Kiev because Doublet was eliminated at Osberton for three refusals at a jump into water.

Doublet had never stopped with Anne before and of all her horses he was the one who really enjoyed jumping into water. They had already been into it twice that day, but after the first, where he jumped very boldly, they landed in a heap as his feet stuck in a soft patch. Later they negotiated a log into the lake, but at the third jump down into water, perhaps frightened of losing his feet in more soft mud, Doublet just simply froze.

At Kiev the going was hard as expected, but the cross-country was beautifully built and none of the riders appeared unduly worried by what became the notorious fence 2. Mark, who had ridden an untried horse of Bertie Hill's to win at Burghley the previous week, was in Kiev to support the British team in general and his fiancée in particular. After walking round he had decided not to bother to watch Anne at that particular fence but to station himself further round the course. Richard Meade, the only man in the team, was unconcerned about it. Anne herself, who had a superb round on the steeplechase, says that basically her trouble at fence 2 was that she had convinced herself there was only one way of jumping it, across the angle, aiming at the middle section where there were most poles over the wide, deep expanse yawning below. It was to be a hard way to learn, but the lesson of that day, never since ignored, is to study all the alternative ways of approaching, and jumping, a cross-country obstacle.

Word started coming back of one or two horses, including Debbie West's Baccarat, the first of the days 35 victims, either eliminated or falling at the second fence; then that the bank in front of the middle section had started to crumble. Anne was told to jump it on the left hand side – and that was an approach she had not considered. She had to turn right-angled after coming along the side of the hill, and she did not go high enough for Goodwill to gather the necessary speed for clearing the spread, especially as they were half a stride out and he had to stand off.

Goodwill gave none of the normal indications of a horse when it thinks it is going to hit a fence, but high up in the air above the rails, just as Anne realised they were not going to make it, he dropped like a stone. His hind legs were already tucked up and when he hit the far rail with his front hooves he crash-landed straight onto his nose.

The Princess says she has never hit the ground so fast or so hard, and she took the main impact on the side of her leg. At the time she was unaware of the shoulder injury which subsequent X-rays showed to be a painful dislocation, but her leg was numb from mid-thigh to mid-calf. She could not stand on it, Goodwill appeared completely dazed, and as she was riding as an individual there seemed little point in going on.

The difference between riding as a member of a team and riding as an individual was something the press chose to ignore when reporting the Princess's retirement alongside the story of Janet Hodgson. She was the heroic team member who crashed at the same fence and then, to save the British team from elimination, continued on her way, bloody-faced and with four teeth hanging by a thread. Some years later the press would be reporting how Princess Anne, concussed from a fall on the cross-country course at the Olympics in Montreal, as a member of the British team insisted on climbing back into the saddle, and completed the course with no subsequent recollection of the last 17 fences.

Anne and Mark both had two horses entered for Badminton in 1974 and their prospects looked bright. By then they were living in a house, one of the many army quarters at Sandhurst where Mark was an instructor, and were enjoying helping each other with the schooling of their horses. It was also a great comfort having each other to see them through the ups and downs of the fortunes of competing, a succour they were both to need at intervals that day.

Three weeks before, Mark had won the advanced class at Liphook on Columbus, and was third with Great Ovation, his two horses separated by Anne and Doublet in second place (Goodwill was going to Badminton as her other ride). They had made their final arrangements at South Molton, taking the horses to Bertie Hill, and with only one groom between them Anne had enjoyed looking after Doublet. It was almost the first time she had dealt with this side of a horse's welfare herself and she had been slightly anxious in case Doublet should not eat or look as well without his usual girl groom. She need not have worried.

At Badminton the horse was looking splendid. He was in the lead at the end of the dressage phase, with Mark second on Great Ovation and equal third with Columbus. Goodwill's test was the only disappointment. He had not pleased the judges and at the end of that phase was lying twenty-seventh. He was then to prove himself with splendid jumping on the steeplechase, the cross-country, and ultimately the show-jumping, that brought Anne up to a creditable fourth in the final placings. It was some compensation for the shattering fall Doublet had at the open ditch on the steeplechase course that caused the Princess, so confident beforehand that her loved horse had at last recovered his previous form, to withdraw him.

Mark was also in need of a morale booster when Great Ovation, his dual Badminton winner, was eliminated with three refusals at the Bullfinch. It was up to Columbus to save Mark's day – and win him that £5 bet made the year before. But as the great horse galloped on his way to victory, ears pricked, clearing fence after fence without a foot wrong, eating up the distance with his lengthy, powerful stride, the thought may have slipped into Mark's mind that here at last was the public proof of what he and Anne had never doubted – that the Queen's horse was a superb and peerless eventer.

Since that day the fortunes have been the usual mixture of disappointments and triumphs, of joys and sorrows, and one or two tragedies. Only a short while after Badminton Princess Anne had to contend with what she has described as 'quite the most ghastly experience' of her life. Mark was away on manoeuvres, and she was cantering Doublet at Windsor when she heard the 'crack!' of his hind leg snapping. There had been no semblance of lameness after the fall at Badminton, not the slightest suspicion of anything being wrong, but afterwards she and Alison came to the conclusion that the horse must have suffered a small star fracture above the hock. Whatever the reason, nothing could be done and Doublet, of whom the Princess once said: 'There is no other one . . .', was immediately put down. In years to come when Prince Charles was to see Allibar lying dead at his feet, his sister would be able fully to understand his feelings.

On that same May Mark won Tidworth with Persian Holiday (Percy for short). It was a victory that, with other wins at Tidworth and Wylye on the loaned Laureate II, at Burghley with the Hill's Maid Marion, and then with Columbus at Badminton, meant he had been unbeaten in British three-day events since the previous year.

In 1974 Mark won his section of the Army Horse Trials at Tidworth with Persian Holiday, while a single mistake with Flame Gun dropped the Princess into second place in her section. The run up to the World Championships at Burghley in the autumn was less propitious. First Mark's old back injury flared up, then Columbus, slightly lame from a knock in the horsebox, could not participate in the final trial at Osberton. In the end Mark was picked for the team and Anne with Goodwill included amongst Britain's eight individuals.

After the cross-country Mark and Columbus were eight points ahead of their nearest rival, the American, Bruce Davidson. A modicum of luck is needed in each phase of an event, but since the show-jumping held no terrors for Columbus, at that point Mark should have been feeling the World Championship was at least within reach. Instead he was suffering the most bitter disappointment of his career.

Unpenalised on the steeplechase course Columbus had continued on round the cross-country clear, and in the fastest time, but at the penultimate of the 32 fences Mark knew something was a little wrong. He thought a leg-bandage had slipped, the horse was not faltering, and they continued the short way on to the finish. But it was not a bandage, it was part of a tendon that had slipped off the horse's hock. Even then there was some hope. They worked all night on the damage and by the next morning Columbus was sound. Then he settled the matter for himself by kicking out at one of the vets and repeating the original damage. As Mark has said, one minute he was riding probably the best horse in the world, the next he was having to realise he might never compete with him again.

Goodwill came twelfth on that eventful day, but not without some anxious moments for his rider and the eventual need of veterinary attention. In retrospect Anne thinks he must have thumped himself very hard on the back of a tendon sheath during the steeplechase. It was not apparent at the time but on the cross-country, with the memory of Doublet only too vivid, the Princess had a frightening round. Goodwill was not lame but he was not his usual self. He was not jumping freely, there was an uncharacteristic refusal at the Double Coffin and nearly a fall at the water. The most alarming feature was the way he nose-dived the drop-fences, not so much jumping as just going straight down off the edge.

Neither Anne nor Mark was sorry to see the end of the 1974 eventing season.

The three months of preparation for Badminton in 1975 were busy ones, especially for the Princess. They had five horses at Sandhurst and with only one girl groom, Anne 'did' two of them herself for the first eight weeks or so. It meant everything from feeding to mucking-out and tack-cleaning but she enjoyed it. She felt she got to know the horses that much better and has often wished since that her public commitments allowed her more time for helping round the stables. Since those days there has usually been one girl groom per two horses, which might indicate a light job. But although the Princess and Mark do all the schooling themselves, involving dressage, jumping, cantering, and galloping, they cannot always be there. When they are not the girls have to extend their normal hours of road work, and do the stable work in the afternoons.

As far as the actual event was concerned the preparations were to prove abortive, as Badminton was, literally, washed out after the first day. But Anne and Mark joined a small contingent of other British riders and flew to the USA, to compete in a three-day event at Ledyard in Massachusetts. It was a very enjoyable experience, although for Mark another disappointment. Laureate II, apparently ready to make a comeback after a year off work, gave Mark a terrible ride both in the steeplechase and in the cross-country, and they were eventually eliminated at the Coffin. The most likely explanation for this untypical débacle was that the horse had got its tongue over the bit. Anne finished tenth on Arthur of Troy, a Thoroughbred that she always felt was a stupid horse, a description that Mark considered sheer heresy, and was to sell in 1977.

That autumn the Princess, with Goodwill, was asked to be a

member of the first all-female team ever chosen by the selectors, to compete for the European Championships at Luhmühlen in West Germany. Despite the trauma of their trail-blazer who was injured in her second fall on the cross-country, the British team returned with the silver team medal, the individual gold won by Lucinda Prior-Palmer on Be Fair, and the individual silver won by Princess Anne on Goodwill.

On the strength of that medal Goodwill, like Be Fair, did not have to compete at Badminton in the following April. 1976 was Olympic year, and Badminton crucial for any rider hoping to prove to the selectors he had a horse of Olympic standard for Montreal. Originally Mark had four horses in the running, Brazil, Persian Holiday and Laureate II, all being prepared at Sandhurst, and a grey mare, Favour, in which he had a half share, and Columbus, doing their initial training with Alison Oliver. Anne had entered Arthur of Troy and, always a favourite, the cocky little Flame Gun, but their impressive first entry soon lost its gilt. Columbus had progressed well after an operation on his tendon, but by March when the work increased he become more unlevel and it had to be accepted his eventing days were presumably over. Both Anne's horses went slightly lame and were withdrawn, and as Mark could only compete with three horses, Laureate II, brilliant but sometimes unpredictable, was dropped.

On the day it transpired that the scores of only two out of Mark's three horses could count and the last one he rode would have to go *hors concours*. It was unfortunate that he had already nominated Persian Holiday, the one he considered had the best chance, for this position.

On the cross-country Brazil lost a shoe, floundered in the lake and then fell over the tree trunk, and was retired after two refusals at the Sunken Road. With a knee damaged in the fall Mark set out again, with Favour, to have a fast clear round and finish the day in third place. Persian Holiday went steadily and well, with just one stop in the lake.

After the usual final selection at Osberton, where Goodwill gave unmistakable proof of his fitness, Princess Anne was included in Britain's Olympic team with Lucinda Prior-Palmer, Hugh Thomas, and Richard Meade. Mark was asked to go as reserve rider, taking Favour and Persian Holiday.

In the days when she was working with Alison Oliver, coming to grips with Doublet, enjoying Purple Star, schooling the young giant Columbus, Anne had nursed the secret, seemingly improbable ambition of one day representing her country in the Olympic equestrian event. At Montreal, with Playamar lamed in his fall with Hugh Thomas and Be Fair with the injury that sadly put paid to his eventing, the British team suffered calamities that put them out of the running. But for Princess Anne Montreal was the place where at least part of her personal dream came true.

In the dressage Goodwill, so exuberant he looked likely to make his exit through the judges' box, collected 91.25 penalties to place them twenty-sixth. On the cross-country, due to a message about a soft

Princess Anne with Doublet at the Burghley Horse Trials.

patch in front of the nineteenth fence that failed to get back in time, the horse got bogged and fell dramatically, but they finished the course. The next day a safe but slow round in the show-jumping gave them twenty-fourth place in the whole event. Maybe the dream would have had the placing higher, but as the Princess said beforehand. 'Being on the short-list I consider to be an achievement; if I get to Montreal I will consider that to be another achievement – and if I actually get a ride, that will be quite something!'

Whether the 1976 Olympics constituted the peak for Princess Anne depends, as she has also said, on whether she finds another horse with the ability of Goodwill. She may have done so – with a young horse it is hard to tell – but in the past six or seven years there has been a change in venue for her and Mark, the realisation of a family, changes in horses and policies, and to some extent in outlook.

The first big change was the move to Gatcombe Park, with Mark leaving the army to take an agricultural course at Cirencester and then turning his hand to farming. The house is not very large and run with a small staff, its most striking feature being the homely, informal atmosphere. The stable block was too restricted, so they built an American-style horse barn. It is an L-shaped building with room for 15, the tack room in the middle in one corner, and the feed room opposite. One of the boxes was constructed as a water-box, at the time described by part of the national press, over-excited on the subject of extravagance, as a horse swimming-pool à l'américaine. It seemed to the Princess a rather high-flown portrayal of a normal sized water-tight box, that can be flooded to the depth of about a foot to relieve tenderness or swelling in a horse's lower leg. In fact, it is more often used for storage. As Anne remarks rather pointedly, because of the 'temporary' three boxes Mark erected in space reserved for storage, the straw has to go into the passage, and the water-box is full of hay.

Their farm is mostly arable, so that riding over much of it is dependent on the season of the year, but there are useful valleys that are not cropped, and quite a considerable block of woodland. They have their own practice cross-country course of a few fences, but there is not a lot of it and parts are too steep even for a horse. The Princess says she keeps asking for some nice little fences for her novice horses, but they do not seem to materialise!

After turning farmer, the second big change for Mark came in 1980 with his sponsorship by Range Rover, now extended until 1983 and with a further two-year option to aid his preparations for the ultimate goal – the 1984 Olympic Games. There are very few three-day event riders at the top today who can afford to keep going without some form of sponsorship – although it must not affect their amateur status. In many countries most sports, including eventing, can rely on government aid. But this does not occur in Britain. Mark is a hard-working farmer running his acreage on a strictly commercial footing, but he does not get paid by the Civil List for his public engagements, there are bills to pay and a mortgage, and his income would not run to keeping high-class event horses.

With one exception all Mark's horses therefore form a Range Rover team and are quite separate from Princess Anne's. The team is a strong one with one or two of high potential. Of the lesser lights, Town and County has been a consistently good horse and although he has not won anything spectacular has taken first place in several one-day events or been amongst the first three. He always tries hard and a muscle enzyme deficiency, now corrected, accounted for his finding life at one time rather hard work. Mark bought Going Places for his team in the summer of 1980 and was rewarded by winning the Midland Bank International Class at Wylye in the following autumn. He took fourth place in the same class with Blizzard II, a tough well-bred novice that was second in the novice championships at Locko Park and seems likely to go far. He is leased to Mark on a personal basis and is, therefore, the 'outsider' amongst the Range Rover horses.

Captain Mark Phillips taking part in the Dressage Competition at Badminton on the Queen's horse Columbus in April 1980.

Princess Anne rode Blizzard when he first arrived but soon decided he would do better with Mark. He was a show-hunter and is a smashing horse, honest as the day is long, and gallops naturally. But he is also very, very fast and when it came to stopping Anne says he made Goodwill 'look like a soft option!' Two young horses were added in 1982 – High Regard and Out and About, the latter formerly ridden by Emma de Hahn and a winner in the novice section at Sherborne with Mark in May.

In 1980 Mark was sixth at Badminton with Lincoln, and won the event with the same horse the following year, a victory that makes him and Lucinda Green (Prior-Palmer) the only two riders to have won Badminton four times. In the irritating way of equines Lincoln then injured himself when turned out for a few day's rest, by putting his leg through the gate when waiting to come in. The damage kept him off work for some months and precluded him from any chance of being selected for the 1981 European Championships.

Mark's chief hope is the good young horse Classic Lines, the winner of the Golden Griffin Trophy in the Midland Bank Novice Championships at Locko Park in 1980 – where Mark also collected third place with another of his team. In 1981 he rode Classic Lines as a member of the winning British team at Hooge Mierde, the three-day event in Holland. There were several more satisfactory placings before an unexpected mishap at Burghley, when the horse lost his footing and fell on the approach to the Lower Trout Hatchery. Honour across country was retrieved at Badminton in 1982 where Classic Lines jumped clear with only 0.8 time penalties, although 20 penalties in the show-jumping gave them fourteenth place at the finish.

At eight years old this big, strong horse not yet in his prime has obvious potential and Mark thinks a lot of him. So do the selection committee who short-listed Mark with Classic Lines for the World Championships at Luhmühlen in September 82. After the amount of previous ill luck it seemed inconceivable that it should dog Mark yet again, but at the moment Classic Lines should have started training he was found to be suffering from a 'flu virus. All the horses at Gatcombe were then tested and although they did not seem to be suffering the blood-tests showed they all had the infection. With no work and being led out to pick at grass each day they recovered very quickly – all except Classic Lines. He had not shown signs of anything being wrong until coughing a couple of times after exercise one morning, and then standing looking 'like a man with 'flu'. The horses are vaccinated each year against horse 'flu, but Classic Lines took much longer to recover because he was exercised when he already had the virus, a different one from normal, and the vaccine had merely masked the symptoms.

Mark knows that the vaccinations, which are compulsory for international horses, are only effective against certain strains of virus. They also seem to lower the animal's body resistance to other strains, making horses more susceptible to the illness and finding it more difficult to throw off the infection.

'Flu at Gatcombe had a side-effect that concerned the aspirations of a group of young riders. It caused the cancellation of one of the three annual Range Rover bursary training courses, two for young riders, one for juniors, who are chosen to come with their horses for a week's schooling under Mark's, very successful, tuition.

In recent years Princess Anne's eventing has been partly programmed by the birth of their two children, Peter born on November 15 1977 and Zara on May 15 1981. Nowadays she takes her 'horse plans' very much as they come along and depending, as always, on how much time she has available. Compared with the time she can spend training, she finds the amount devoted to it by other competitors almost frightening. Some years ago it did not seem to matter so much, but now the competition has grown so fierce she sometimes wonders why she bothers to turn up! The Princess considers she has got more selective in her material as she gets older – now she *knows* what she wants from a horse and is no longer prepared to accept anything else, whereas before she was usually prepared to go on trying with an animal, hoping some of it might come right. Now she has been doing it long enough to know what constitutes a good horse, and that is what she is after. If she does not find one with what she considers to be the right qualities, and they are not easy to come by, she does not bother with it.

In 1982 the Princess had one or two promising youngsters and Stevie B. He was the attractive young chestnut that the Queen bought from the same source as Goodwill. He appeared to have the qualities Princess Anne requires and did consistently well with her in one-day events, and when she was one of the members of the winning British team in the three-day event at Hooge Mierde in May 82. To the public who saw Stevie B fall in the Trout Hatchery with the Princess at Burghley in 1981, and descend into the lake at Badminton with her in the following April, it might have appeared the horse had a problem with water. But as Anne knew very well, it was curiosity rather than water that was Stevie B's downfall on those two occasions. He never made a mistake jumping water at other events where there were few spectators, including the one in Holland where there was plenty of it, with a complex of water obstacles that caused some trouble to other horses. At Burghley and Badminton the crowds are enormous and tend to congregate at those two water jumps. The Princess described the horse as a 'peery' character, far too interested in people – and inattention when asked to cope with the

A dramatic picture of Captain Mark Phillips showjumping on Classic Lines at Badminton in June 1982.

intricacies of jumping over an obstacle and down into water is a recipe for disaster. She did not know whether Stevie B would ever get over his curiosity syndrome sufficiently to be really first class – as he can be at the events that do not attract the crowds and decide to concentrate on the galloping and jumping for which he has considerable ability. Eventually she made the decision to sell him to a junior rider.

The Princess and Mark no longer do very much team-jumping across country because their present horses do not need it. They used to do it with the novice horses in the spring, and sometimes with older horses in the autumn, but only with those likely to benefit from the experience. They think the sport can teach novices to manage themselves correctly across country, to 'think on their feet' even better than with hunting, for which there is seldom time and is a sport that does not necessarily 'open a horse out'. Team jumping can be especially good for novice horses that are 'pokey' before jumping instead of going on at their fences. They decide they want to keep up with the other horses and suddenly find they can jump at speed, that it is not as difficult as it looks – but the courses have to be carefully chosen.

A week with Bertie Hill before Badminton is always a 'must' and they wish they could manage such visits more often. Anne feels that outside help can provide the necessary stimulus, and that a critical eye can be very beneficial, but it is impossible to fit in visits more frequently and they do all their own schooling. It has always been helpful to ride each other's horses, when Mark can use his strength and weight to sort out one of Anne's that is being unco-operative, and her more calming approach is excellent if one of his is being extra-sensitive.

If a young horse fails to grow or proves no good for eventing it is sold on, but making and selling horses is not part of the Gatcombe set-up. Princess Anne now possesses the minimum number of horses for her requirements, and as far back as 1977 was complying with the Queen's wish to cut down wherever possible. Mardi Gras was one of those she parted with at that time, an amusing young horse she had upgraded to advanced standard that was a descendant of the Queen Mother's great horse, Manicou.

When age obliges a parting with the older horses, provision is always made for these long-standing friends to enjoy their remaining years. Anne's good pony High Jinks stayed well and happy with a family on the Balmoral estate until 1980, when a septic corn that did not respond to treatment necessitated his being put down.

Goodwill was 14 when he went to Badminton for the last time in 1979. The cross-country that day was as usual fair and beautifully constructed but it called for the speed and flair of a good, bold horse, and Goodwill responded nobly. When the delighted Princess came in she was cheerfully acknowledging that her horse had been in command all the way round and that all she had to do was steer, but it was the rider's as well as the horse's experience that was needed to take them round without penalty. Rather more than Goodwill's usual exuberance in the dressage arena had exacted 84.2 penalties and he collected 5 more in the show-jumping, but that superb exhibition of faultless jumping across country brought the Princess sixth place at the finish, and retirement with honour for Goodwill.

That autumn Anne rode him in one or two cross-country team races and then tried hunting him. Apart from one very good day with the Wynnstay, this was not an unqualified success and the Princess is being literal when she says she and her horse 'rather got carried away!' In the heyday of his eventing, although Goodwill was very stable, could not be described as a tear-away and was not fast enough really to pull, for some while his rider was at odds with him about stopping. Out hunting his jumping is always splendid but Anne did not find him exactly amusing to hunt. Unlike other horses he seems not to notice when the field is slowing down or stopping, and if people halt in a gateway to wait Goodwill simply carries on through them. He does not pull or gallop any faster in an effort to catch up, he just does not see any point in halting and evinces no interest in the idea. It was thought he might be all right as a Master's horse where he would anyway be out in front, and in 1980 he was offered in that capacity to Bertie Hill, one of the best of horsemen. It had been pointed out to Bertie that it would unlikely to be worthwhile taking Goodwill out except when he was hunting hounds – and eventually his new rider came to acknowledge the good sense of that advice!

Goodwill remained in Devon for the 1980 season but, sadly, at the end developed a 'big leg' that the vet thought should preclude him from the exertions of a Master's horse. He returned to Gatcombe and was then turned out. In the autumn of 81, when he was 16, there was some thought of hunting him 'off grass' to see if that might improve the old horse's braking system.

The story of Columbus's last fling before retiring as a royal hack, is one that gives Anne and Mark the greatest pleasure. Mark began riding him again in 1977. Against all predictions he became and remained completely sound. In 1979 he demonstrated the fact irrefutably when Mark rode him on a workmanlike round of some of the Grand National fences, for the BBC's preview of the great race on the programme *Grandstand*. Not long afterwards Mark and Columbus joined Princess Anne and Goodwill in the line-up for the Badminton three-day event.

April 21 was the Queen's birthday, and she could not have had a better present than watching the way her two horses, both aged 14, acquitted themselves on that day. Everyone was wondering how Columbus's damaged hock would stand up to the rigours of the course, but both he and Goodwill, the oldest horses there, were to show what good care and good sense can do in the preservation of the necessary physical and mental qualities. Mark and Colombus appeared to float effortlessly round the course, undulating over the fences without interrupting the rhythm of the horse's stride. Goodwill's round on the cross-country that day was superb; Columbus's was described as an epic.

His dressage had been ebullient but not as irrepressible as

Goodwill's, and when he went clear over the show-jumps there was nothing to add to his 66 penalties in the first phase. Mark and Columbus came third on the Badminton score-sheet, and his rider's summing up – 'they don't make many like him . . .' – was the old horse's valediction to the eventing world.

Princess Anne and Captain Mark Phillips leaving Badminton House Stables, the Princess looking elegant in competition dressage outfit.

In 1980 Mark rode Persian Holiday in the Midland Bank Horse Trials Championships at Locko Park to take fifth place and then took second at Burghley after knocking down the first fence in the show-jumping. In age he knew his horse was reaching the end of his eventing days but in 1981, after much deliberation, decided to give him a final fling at Badminton before retirement. When 'Percy' fell at the Quarry, Mark felt he had 'let an old friend down', but the horse was none the worse. Now Persian Holiday, a horse prone to leg troubles but Mark's partner in so many eventing successes, is happily installed with his parents as a hunter.

Like all event-riders the Princess and Mark have been well aware of the criticism levelled at some of the three-day event courses and fences for being too severe. They feel that on the whole the courses are good, and the occasional bad fences are usually made so by the outside influence of weather and/or terrain. They themselves have never withdrawn their horses after inspecting a course because they felt the fences were asking too much. On the other hand they do feel that a number of falls and eliminations are due to horses being upgraded too quickly and therefore faced with courses for which they are not ready. They also feel strongly that some riders fail to realise just how much a three-day event takes out of a horse, and enter for too many competitions. As for the future, they think eventing will continue in its present form, the outlook as rosy as for any other equestrian sport.

On a more personal future note, if Princess Anne is asked if she intends teaching her children to ride the answer is likely to be 'no' – at any rate not for some years yet. There are no pressures about the matter. Zara is too young, and although Peter is used to having horses around and going to some of the events with his parents, until quite late in 1981 he was not very enthusiastic about riding himself. Then suddenly for no particular reason he was 'on' the idea and became quite keen. After receiving a special Christmas present from his paternal grandmother, it does seem likely that Peter may well carry on the traditional link with horses.

Mrs Phillips' flair for helping nervous riders is matched by her one for finding the right horse or pony for the right situation. Her present to her grandson was a 12.2-hand, part-bred Welsh Mountain pony that had won the Lloyds Bank Riding for the Disabled Trophy at the 1981 Horse of the Year Show at Wembley. This ensures temperament and manners, and by July 1982 the pale palomino, Trigger, had proved himself to be a 'real gentleman' and was definitely 'quite popular'.

Chapter Twelve

Equestrianism: The Family Tradition

WHEN TRIGGER first arrived at Gatcombe Park Peter, his new owner was four years old, the same age as his uncle, Prince Andrew, had been in 1964 when he was enjoying what the Queen aptly described as an 'association' with a Shetland pony.

The Prince has not ridden since shooting and sailing, rugger and other school games and sports took priority when he was at Gordonstoun, but as a small boy he had fun with Valkyrie both at Windsor, and at Balmoral where his pony used to arrive in a wooden crate after coming north by train.

The little black mare was presented to the Queen in 1960 by the people of the Shetland Isles, and was then a yearling. Eventually she was broken in, to both saddle and harness, at Windsor. Andrew normally 'rode' his pony, but enjoyed the occasional drive out in the donkey barouche that was a Christmas present, in 1846, to Queen Victoria's children from Queen Adelaide, Consort of William IV.

Some years after Valkyrie went to stud, Andrew formed a liaison with one of Prince Philip's ex-polo ponies, and liked charging about the grounds at Balmoral with an animal that was elderly but still satisfyingly fast. That was a time when Princess Anne refused to take her young brother out riding because she said: 'It's instant death – he always falls off when he's with me!'

Although Prince Edward has not had the time or quite the same inclination to take his riding as seriously as Princess Anne, it is a sport he thoroughly enjoys and one he was hoping to be able to continue during the time spent in New Zealand. In the early days he occasionally sought the company of a diminutive pony called Mr Dinkum, who was then superseded by something a little larger, a popular New Forest dun pony called Duncan. For the past few years the Prince has been having a lot of fun with Princess Anne's 'hand-downs', Purple Star and Flame Gun, and Reneau the Algerian Barb. He is a good and keen rider and sometimes competes at novice level. In April 1981, he and his cousins, Princess Margaret's children Lord Linley and Lady Sarah Armstrong-Jones, enjoyed themselves 'having a go' in a minor jumping competition at Ascot.

Princess Margaret rode a lot as a child, and continued to do so until quite recently. In those early months of the war when she and Princess Elizabeth stayed on in Scotland and looked after their own

Jockey Eph Smith touches his cap to the Queen and Princess Margaret in the paddock after his victory on Snow Cat in the Rous Memorial Stakes at Ascot in 1958.

ponies, Margaret had as much fun with Hans, her dun-coloured Norwegian pony, as Elizabeth did with Jock. The Princesses rode a great deal together as they grew up but usually developed different preferences amongst the riding horses in the Windsor Mews. Princess Margaret did not share the Queen's regard for Betsy, whose character transcended her breeding, or for other cross-bred personalities such as the half-Russian, Cossack. She much preferred Thoroughbreds and the ex-racehorses, Agreement and Worcran, were two of her favourites.

Riding during the annual holiday at Balmoral is always one of the chosen recreations for most of the royal family, and for Princess Margaret it was especially enjoyable when her children were old enough to join in. At the time when Sarah was sharing Mr Dinkum with her cousin Edward, David, Lord Linley, had graduated to his own pony Buttercup. His first acquaintance with a pony was in the days when the Queen was showing Andrew how to handle Valkyrie and taking him out around the castle grounds. David was often one of the party, either sharing the pony, with occasional squabbles when one or other of the riders did not wish to get off, or pedalling his tricycle in pursuit of one of the policemen patrolling the grounds. As he got older his liking for speed was satisfied either by the 'go-karts' he and his cousins raced round the Balmoral paths, or by riding at a pace that was a source of worry to the family groom doing his best to keep up. By then Buttercup had been succeeded by the 14.1-hand Robin and Sarah had her little Arabian horse, Prince Azure, both animals brought up to Balmoral from Windsor where they were normally housed.

Although the Duke and Duchess of Gloucester do not keep horses of their own they do ride from time to time, and as their children grow older the stables and riding facilities at their home, Barnwell Manor, may well be in use again.

When Princess Alice, Duchess of Gloucester, and the late Duke lived at Barnwell (they bought the house in 1937), they hunted with the Fitzwilliam Hounds. The Duke gave up hunting after the war but there were polo ponies to hack and the Duchess sometimes took their sons, Prince William and Prince Richard, to local cubbing meets. Later, until his death in 1972 in an aircrash, Prince William kept his own string of polo ponies and played regularly, both in Nigeria when he was Third Secretary at the British High Commission in Lagos and at Windsor when he returned to England.

Princess Alice has ridden all her life and started hunting at the age of ten, in Scotland with the Duke of Buccleuch's hounds, her father's pack, and then with the Woodland Pytchley in Northamptonshire. In the early nineteen-thirties she hunted in India and in Kenya where she also rode in point-to-points. At the end of the World War II, when the Duke of Gloucester was Governor-General in Australia, he and Princess Alice kept horses at Canberra and rode whenever they could, including the opportunities offered when visiting cattle stations. With such a background of horses and riding Princess Alice is sure to encourage her

LEFT: *Princess Margaret pats prizewinner Windsor Romany Lass at the National Pony Show in 1950.*

RIGHT: *The Duke and Duchess of Gloucester riding with the Woodland Pytchley Hunt in November 1935.*

grandchildren to take up a sport that has always given her such pleasure.

The Duke of Kent attends such ceremonial occasions as Trooping the Colour on horseback, usually riding a grey police horse called Richard, but otherwise he and the Duchess seldom ride nowadays. Their elder son, the Earl of St Andrews, does not ride but the younger children, Lady Helen Windsor and Lord Nicholas Windsor, do so occasionally. In Norfolk they share two ponies, William and Romany, with the local vicar's children.

A long time ago Princess Alexandra, the Duke's sister, frequently rode some of the horses in the Royal Mews at Windsor. Now pressure of work would not allow the Princess and her husband, Mr Angus Ogilvie, to list riding as more than an occasional recreation, but as a child and before marriage Alexandra rated riding as one of her top pleasures. She has always been a very good horsewoman and like other members of the royal family considers the sport to be one of the best methods of 'unwinding' in a life of public duty. Her son, James, does not ride, but her daughter, Marina, has inherited her mother's keenness. She belongs to the local Pony Club and competes in the shows and events.

Unlike Princess Alexandra, her younger brother, Prince Michael of Kent, did not count horses amongst his interests until a few years ago. As a child he rode a little but not with much enjoyment and although he joined a regiment, the 11th Hussars, that despite mechanisation remains, in a private capacity, very horse orientated, Prince Michael's recreation took the form of the hazardous, break-neck speeds of bob-sleighing at international level.

Horses caught up with the Prince after he met his wife, then Baroness Marie-Christine von Reibnitz. At the time she had a much

Princess Alexandra presenting the cup to the winner of the Children's Pony Event at Aldershot Horse Show in 1946.

loved Anglo-Arab mare that she rode daily in Richmond Park, and in order to meet without undue publicity it seemed Prince Michael would have to take to horseback as well. He borrowed a horse from a stable at Richmond Park but the venture was not an unqualified success. The horse was not entirely a beginner's ride and did little to increase its rider's liking for equines. This attitude was changed when the Prince and Princess were given the opportunity to ride horses of the Household Cavalry on early morning exercise, a pleasure they are still able to enjoy. It was an offer made originally after the Princess, only the day before her son was born, saw her beloved mare involved in a horrifying accident with a car that necessitated the horse being put down.

By 1981 Prince and Princess Michael at last found the country house they wanted in the Cotswolds, and discovered hunting to be part of the everyday scene in that area. The idea appealed to both of them, and when Prince Michael came out of the Army at the beginning of that year he decided to spend the month of rehabilitation, offered to those who leave the service, on a riding course at Melton Mowbray. As a natural athlete with excellent balance he adapted easily to a sport he found to be most enjoyable, especially when he started jumping.

Princess Michael rode as a child, on every possible occasion and on anything that was available, but without having instruction as such. It was what she calls 'rough riding', starting with the tough little Haflinger ponies, adept at bucking their riders off over their heads, or, when staying with friends in the country seizing any opportunity to ride out and help bring in the cattle. The instruction came later when she was about 16 and visited South West Africa.

That was when Marie-Christine had the chance of spending six months on a beautiful cattle ranch where they also bred horses. These were half-breds by a stallion of Hungarian/Arab/Trackehnen blood crossed with Irish hunters for strength and stamina, that were proving very successful for three-day eventing, or 'the military' as it was called. With the other young people there she rode for three hours each morning in an outdoor school, instructed by a wonderful old lady whose physical disabilities, only too apparent when she was dismounted, could not be believed once she was on a horse. For the first time, the Princess says she was given some understanding of the art of riding and of what it is all about – although she insists she has not really progressed much further since! But it was exciting that, at a very elementary level, she and the other pupils were able to compete in a few minor one-day events.

One summer before marriage Princess Michael was able to join a course for young people, invited to the Lipizzaner stud to help keep the young horses exercised while the professional trainers were on holiday. The attributes, both physical and mental, of this famous breed made an unforgettable impression, as did the rock-face scored by millions of hooves over which the young horses were chased each day to ensure the strength of leg and tendon for which Lipizzaners are renowned. But other than these two opportunities the Princess has had little training in the art of dressage, an omission she sadly regrets.

By the end of the summer of 1981 the Prince and Princess and their children were installed in their country home for the long weekends. There are three horses in the stables, one weight-carrying, level-headed hunter, found with the helpful advice of Sir John Miller, for the Prince, and two big, good-looking blacks with excellent manners and a kind eye for the Princess, all in the charge of their indispensable girl groom. The plans for hunting that season were well under way, although there had been a small problem or two due to their being complete newcomers to the sport, and to the Princess's occasional misunderstanding of some hunting terms. She had found it very puzzling to be told she and her husband needed to get 'rat-catcher' (informal dress) before going cub-hunting – as she *knew* their stables were free of rodents!

The Princess was very keen to learn to ride side-saddle. It was a form of equitation that had appealed to her for a long time and she was delighted when Sir John's niece, Sylvia Stanier, offered to help. An expert in the art, she was in London for the annual schooling of Burmese she undertakes for the Queen before the Trooping the Colour, and was able to give Princess Michael some lessons in the indoor school at the palace. This help was continued in the country in the autumn of 1981, after an interval before the birth of the Princess's second child. After some initial difficulty in finding a suitable saddle, Princess Michael was hoping to become sufficiently proficient to be able to hunt side-saddle that first season, as she truly believes it to be a safer method of riding, and one making falls less likely.

Prince and Princess Michael's horse interests are not confined to hunting. In addition to riding twice a week in Hyde Park in the early morning when in London, they thoroughly enjoy riding round the country-side near their home in the Cotswolds. The Prince also shares his wife's ambition to own a suitable pony or horse to drive, both for fun and perhaps under the auspices of the British Driving Society. Princess Michael has always loved driving from the days when she drove sleighs on the snow-covered roads round her Austrian home, and thinks her strong feeling for it stems from being half-Hungarian, a nation that excels at the art.

Another ambition is to own an Arabian horse. The Princess's much loved Anglo-Arab had much of the personality of her Arab ancestry, and the desert breed is admired for its visual beauty and versatility. As President of the British Arab Horse Society Princess Michael hopes to help in persuading more of the general public that an Arabian horse can race, hunt and jump, do excellent dressage, and go in harness, in addition to being lovely to look at.

Both she and Prince Michael are insistent that they are amateurs in the horse world, but their keenness and interest is apparent. Their children are as yet very young, but no doubt ponies will appear on the scene in due course, especially as Princess Michael has now become Patron of Ponies of Great Britain.

Prince Edward riding Reneau out in the grounds at Badminton.

A Final Word

FOR ANYONE who has had the privilege, and the fun, of delving into the varied horse interests of the royal family it is apparent that the traditional link between horses and the throne is perfectly safe for the present. And, as far as one dare hazard a guess about anything in this rapidly changing world, the future bond looks secure as well.

It also comes over very clearly just how important horses and ponies are to a family who, in varying degrees, lead lives of demanding public duty, but ideal relaxation is not all that the animals offer. The Queen gets as much amusement out of her horses' foibles, as interest in trying to sort them out. None of the royal family is in the least pompous in their attitudes to their various animals, echoing Prince Philip's truism: 'The horse is a great leveller and anyone who is concerned about his dignity would be well advised to keep away from horses.' He was also quoting from experience when he wrote in an article, in 1977: 'Having a family which seems to be equally willing to be humiliated by the horse, I have to live with the expectation that they too will suffer injury and indignity. The only advantage of the personal experience of this sort of thing is that I am not surprised when it happens to them, and I am full of sympathy and advice for treatment and recovery. . . .'

The Queen Mother likes putting on old clothes and going along to the training stables with her pockets full of apples for her 'darling boys'. Prince Charles cannot help himself becoming emotionally involved with his horses and polo-ponies. The surest place to find Princess Anne in the early hours before an event is either on the road, her HGV licence enabling her to act as co-driver with Mark of their big horsebox, or in the stables on her knees sewing bandages on the legs of a horse.

Coupled with the enjoyment and other good things the royal family receive from their connections with horses, the horse world benefits greatly from the royal interests. Wherever the Queen travels, at home or abroad, and meets members of the horse-racing community, she impresses the experts by her extensive and accurate knowledge of Thoroughbreds and their pedigrees. And it is her genuine and obvious enjoyment of all facets of the racing scene that has been and remains a great boost to British flat-racing. But the Queen's horse interests extend to cover almost all aspects of the equestrian world and this has helped foster the large and rapidly growing numbers of people, young and old

An informal portrait of Princess Anne and Captain Mark Phillips at Locko Park near Derby in August 1980.

and from all stratas of society, who are finding that horses and ponies offer a pleasurable pastime.

After the war it was Prince Philip's enthusiasm for playing polo that, contrary to probability, helped revive a game now being played at many different levels. When he was instrumental in evolving the competitive driving he then took up as his own hobby, he put driving 'on the map' in Britain to an extent no-one could possibly have expected or prophesied.

Prince Charles's polo-playing has continued the good work begun by his father in popularising the game. He was more or less in at the beginning of team racing across country and helped get that sport going. His short flirtation and one that he seems determined to re-kindle, with National Hunt racing, has joined forces with Queen Elizabeth's involvement to aid the 'poor relation' of the racing world.

For some time after Princess Anne started eventing there were still sections of the press who referred to her 'show-jumping' – an indication of how little was then known of this tough and rewarding sport. No doubt with time it would have become more widely recognised, but without the novelty of the Queen's daughter participating in such a rigorous activity and her guts and determination in getting to the top, it is doubtful if the media would have discovered what good television a three-day event can be, or if the general public would have become so interested.

During the past decade or so equestrianism has grown enormously in volume and in complexity. People give all kinds of reasons for owning, riding, or driving horses or ponies. Too often in this competitive world the only one that matters, a genuine liking for horses, becomes blurred by human greed and ambition, material gain, prestige, and prizes.

The royal family have got it right. They have horses and ponies because they are really fond of them and whatever they do with them, they do it for fun.

The Queen and her sister Princess Margaret chatting happily during the Badminton Horse Trials in 1957.